COOK SMART easy everyday

Easy recipes in 30 minutes or less, all updated with *ProPoints®* values

SIMON &
SCHUSTER

London · New York · Sydney · Toronto

A CBS COMPANY

First published in Great Britain by Simon & Schuster UK Ltd, 2011
A CBS Company

Copyright © 2011, Weight Watchers International, Inc.
Simon & Schuster Illustrated Books, Simon & Schuster UK Ltd, First Floor, 222 Gray's Inn Road, London WC1X 8HB

Weight Watchers Publications: Jane Griffiths, Donna Watts, Imogen Prescott and Nina McKerlie

Recipes written by: Sue Ashworth, Sue Beveridge, Tamsin Burnett-Hall, Cas Clarke, Siân Davies, Roz Denny, Becky Johnson, Kim Morphew, Joy Skipper, Penny Stephens and Wendy Veale, as well as Weight Watchers Leaders and Members.

Photography by: Iain Bagwell, Steve Baxter, Steve Lee and Juliet Piddington.
Design and typesetting by Tiger Media Ltd.
Printed and bound in China.

A CIP catalogue for this book is available from the British Library

ISBN 978-0-85720-175-1

1 3 5 7 9 10 8 6 4 2

Pictured on the front cover: Vegetable Spring Rolls with Sweet Chilli Sauce p72, Spanish Rice p40, Steak and Shallots in Red Wine p92, Paradise Pudding p132.
Pictured on the introduction: Spiced Lamb Steaks with Couscous p86, Cheesy Broccoli Soup p62, Eggs Benedict p10, Cranberry and Almond Cookies p154.

 ProPoints® value logo: You'll find this easy to read *ProPoints* value logo on every recipe throughout this book. The logo represents the number of *ProPoints* values per serving each recipe contains. It is not an indication of the fillingness of a recipe.

Weight Watchers *ProPoints* Weight Loss System is a simple way to lose weight. As part of the Weight Watchers *ProPoints* plan you'll enjoy eating delicious, healthy, filling foods that help to keep you feeling satisfied for longer and in control of your portions.

V This symbol denotes a vegetarian recipe and assumes that, where relevant, free range eggs, vegetarian cheese, vegetarian virtually fat free fromage frais, vegetarian low fat crème fraîche and vegetarian low fat yogurts are used. Virtually fat free fromage frais, low fat crème fraîche and low fat yogurts may contain traces of gelatine so they are not always vegetarian. Please check the labels.

✱ This symbol denotes a dish that can be frozen.

Recipe notes
Egg size: Medium, unless otherwise stated.
All fruits and vegetables: Medium sized, unless otherwise stated.
Raw eggs: Only the freshest eggs should be used. Pregnant women, the elderly and children should avoid recipes with eggs that are not fully cooked or raw.
Stock: Stock cubes used in recipes, unless otherwise stated. These should be prepared according to packet instructions.
Recipe timings: These are approximate and meant to be guidelines. Please note that the preparation time includes all the steps up to and following the main cooking time(s).
Microwaves: Timings and temperatures are for a standard 800 W microwave. If necessary, adjust to your own microwave.
Low fat spread: Where a recipe states to use a low fat spread, a light spread with a fat content of no less than 38% should be used.

Contents

Introduction

Tasty, healthy and easy to create – all the recipes in *Cook Smart Easy Everyday* can be made in 30 minutes or less, giving you plenty of time with family and friends even at the end of a busy day. In addition, all recipes have been updated to work with the ***ProPoints* plan**. From quick ideas for brunch to recipes that are perfect for a special supper with friends, there is something here for every day, proving that you don't need hours to create delicious meals.

About Weight Watchers

For more than 40 years Weight Watchers has been helping people around the world to lose weight using a long term sustainable approach. Weight Watchers successful weight loss system is based on four tried and trusted principles:

- Eating healthily
- Being more active
- Adjusting behaviour to help weight loss
- Getting support in weekly meetings

Our unique ***ProPoints*** system empowers you to manage your food plan and make wise recipe choices for a healthier, happier you.

Cooking with Flavour

If you are going to cook healthy, nutritious meals, it is worth investing in some quality ingredients. Although this may be more expensive, the flavour will be better and you will enjoy your food far more. And if you enjoy what you eat, you are more likely to cook more rather than reach for a takeaway menu.

Make the most of seasonal ingredients. From vibrant winter cabbages to spring asparagus, from juicy summer fruit to autumnal squashes, seasonal fresh fruit and vegetables taste far better than frozen or canned. And by ringing the changes you'll be eating a greater variety of fruit and vegetables throughout the year. You'll be less likely to get bored with the same old meals and may even find new favourite ingredients.

Fish is seasonal too. Buy fresh fish and seafood at the fish counter in your supermarket or from a fishmonger. Ask your fishmonger what's in season and smell before you buy. Fresh fish should smell fresh – not fishy – the eyes should be bright and the scales shiny.

When buying meat, always choose lean cuts or lean mince. Consider visiting your local butcher rather than buying from the supermarket – your butcher will know which cuts are best for you and will be able to prepare them the way you want. If you are buying precooked sliced meat, always buy it fresh from the deli counter. Prepacked cooked meat usually has salt and preservatives added.

Even changing staple foods like pasta and rice can increase flavour. Try imported dried pastas, which have a wheaty, bread-like taste and will stay al dente better than most other brands. Or swap plain white rice for basmati or jasmine rice and see the difference. Try some different varieties to find the one you like the most.

Worth Buying

It is worth keeping a few quality basics in your store cupboard that will add extra flavour to your dishes. This way you'll always have ingredients to create a tasty meal.

- Olive oil – a good quality extra virgin olive oil adds a wonderful flavour to dressings. Try a few brands to find one you like.

- Balsamic vinegar – balsamic vinegar is light and fruity. Buy the best you can afford and try it drizzled over salads or vegetables.

- Porcini mushrooms – these mushrooms have an intense flavour but fresh ones are only available at certain times of the year. However dried porcini mushrooms are just as good and are available all year round. They are incredibly versatile and worth stocking for adding to stews, pasta and risottos.

- Parmesan cheese – if you are going to add a little cheese, it is worth making sure it is the best you can afford. Avoid cheap but tasteless ready grated Parmesan and buy a block of Parmigiano-Reggiano instead. You can use a vegetable peeler to create shavings and the flavour will be well worth the extra expense.

- Honey – a drizzle of honey can make all the difference to a pancake or dessert. Specialist honey has a flavour from the region in which it is produced, or from the flower or trees that the bees have predominantly visited. Try a few different types and you'll be amazed at the difference in flavour.

- Chocolate – a little goes a long way with chocolate, but only if you use quality brands. Look for at least 70% cocoa solids – the stronger the chocolate taste, the less you will need.

Storing and Freezing

Once you have mastered the art of cooking delicious meals, you may want to make extra and store or freeze it for a later date. Store any leftovers in sealed containers in the fridge and use them up within a day or two. Many recipes can be frozen, as can individual ingredients, but it is important to make sure you know how to freeze safely.

- Wrap any food to be frozen in rigid containers or strong freezer bags. This is important to stop foods contaminating each other or getting freezer burn.

- Label the containers or bags with the contents and date – your freezer should have a star marking that tells you how long you can keep different types of frozen food.

- Never freeze warm food – always let it cool completely first.

- Never freeze food that has already been frozen and defrosted.

- Freeze food in portions, then you can take out as little or as much as you need each time.

- Defrost what you need in the fridge, making sure you put anything that might have juices, such as meat, on a covered plate or in a container.

Fresh food, such as raw meat or fish, should be wrapped and frozen as soon as possible. Most fruit and vegetables can be frozen by open freezing. Lay them out on a tray and freeze until solid, then pack them into bags. Some vegetables, such as peas, broccoli and broad beans can be blanched first by cooking for 2 minutes in boiling water. Drain and refresh under cold water then freeze once cold. Fresh herbs are great frozen – either seal leaves in bags or, for soft herbs such as basil and parsley, chop finely and add to ice cube trays with water. These are great for dropping into casseroles or soups straight from the freezer.

Some things cannot be frozen. Whole eggs do not freeze well, but yolks and whites can be frozen separately. Vegetables with a high water content, such as salad leaves, celery and cucumber, will not freeze. Fried foods will be soggy if frozen, and sauces such as mayonnaise will separate when thawed and should not be frozen.

Brunches
and Lunches

Get the day off to a great start with something a bit different, like Crunchy Nectarine
Yogurt Pots or a classic Brunch, or ring the changes at lunchtime with a Florentine
Pizza or Mediterranean Vegetable and Pesto Filling.

Start the day as you
mean to go on

Eggs Benedict

Hopefully you'll have a little more time at weekends to prepare breakfast, so can try this tasty variation on bacon and eggs. It's great for weekend guests too.

Serves 2

15 g (½ oz) Hollandaise sauce
1 tablespoon vinegar
2 x 25 g (1 oz) lean bacon medallions
1 beef tomato
1 English style white muffin, split in half
2 eggs
½ tablespoon chopped fresh parsley

---

6 *ProPoints* values per serving
13 *ProPoints* values per recipe

259 calories per serving

Takes **15 minutes**

not recommended

1 Preheat the grill to a medium heat. Place two ovenproof plates in the oven and turn to Gas Mark 1/140°C/fan oven 120°C. Spoon the Hollandaise sauce into a small ramekin dish and pop in the oven on the plates to warm through. (If you don't have a separate grill, you can warm the plates by putting them in a bowl of clean hot water until you need them. The sauce heats in seconds in a microwave). Meanwhile, bring a pan of water to a gentle simmer then add the vinegar.

2 Grill the bacon medallions for a minute or two on each side. Cut the beef tomato so that you have two thick slices and grill these until warmed through. Grill the muffin halves until lightly toasted. Top the muffin halves with the bacon and tomato slices and keep them warm on the prepared plates.

3 Meanwhile, break an egg into a bowl and then slide it gently into the simmering water. Repeat with the other egg and poach for 4 minutes or until the eggs are cooked to your liking.

4 Remove the eggs from the water with a slotted spoon and transfer on to the bacon and tomato-topped muffin halves. Top with the warm Hollandaise sauce, sprinkle with parsley and serve immediately.

Tips Smoked bacon medallions are simply the leanest part of a bacon rasher with all visible fat removed.

Hollandaise sauce can be difficult to make. However, the ready-made version in jars is excellent and is a real time saver.

Variation For a vegetarian option, miss out the bacon medallion – the *ProPoints* values will remain the same.

Classic Omelette

Omelettes are the original fast food – and they're so nutritious and tasty.

Serves 2

4 eggs
4 tablespoons skimmed milk
2 teaspoons butter
200 g (7 oz) low fat soft cheese
2 tablespoons chopped fresh chives, coriander or parsley
salt and freshly ground black pepper
salad leaves, to serve

1 Beat the eggs and milk together. Season.

2 Heat 1 teaspoon of butter in a small, non stick frying pan. Pour in half the egg mixture and cook over a medium high heat until the base sets. Using a wooden spatula, push the cooked egg towards the middle of the pan, so that the uncooked egg flows over the surface, allowing it to set.

3 Spoon half the cheese along the centre of the omelette, letting it melt for a moment or two. Sprinkle with half the chives, coriander or parsley. Fold the omelette over and slide it out on to a warm plate. Keep it in a warm place while you cook the second omelette.

4 Serve the omelettes with the salad leaves.

8 *ProPoints* values per serving
16 *ProPoints* values per recipe

C **365 calories** per serving

Takes **10 minutes**

V

✱ not recommended

Variations Use low fat soft cheese flavoured with garlic and herbs, if you like, for the same *ProPoints* values.

Add a sliced tomato to each omelette before spooning in the cheese.

You could omit the soft cheese altogether and just use sliced tomatoes and chopped fresh herbs. The *ProPoints* values will be reduced to 5 per serving.

Crunchy Nectarine Yogurt Pots

These little fruity pots provide a fresh and healthy start to the day.

Serves 4

4 ripe nectarines or peaches, stoned and quartered
2 pieces pared lemon rind
4 tablespoons honey

300 g (10½ oz) 0% fat Greek yogurt
4 tablespoons granola

1 Place the nectarines or peaches in a small lidded pan with the lemon rind and pour over 200 ml (7 fl oz) water. Bring to the boil, cover and simmer for 5 minutes until the fruit is just soft. Drizzle over the honey and set aside to cool completely.

2 Take four serving glasses, place two pieces of fruit in the base of each and cover with 2 heaped tablespoons of the yogurt then ½ tablespoon of granola. Repeat, ending with the granola.

6 *ProPoints* values per serving
24 *ProPoints* values per recipe

C **198 calories** per serving

Takes **10 minutes** + cooling

V

＊ not recommended

Tip Poached fruit will keep covered in the fridge for up to 3 days.

Variation You could try this with eight small or four large plums, instead of the nectarines, as an alternative. The *ProPoints* values will remain the same.

Banana Pancakes with Maple Syrup

Sometimes you need to push the boat out. So, for something different, try these delicious pancakes to start the day.

Serves 4

50 g (1¾ oz) plain flour
½ teaspoon baking powder
½ teaspoon bicarbonate of soda
¼ teaspoon salt
½ teaspoon sugar
1 banana
1 egg, separated
1 teaspoon low fat spread
150 ml (5 fl oz) buttermilk
low fat cooking spray
2 tablespoons maple syrup

3 ProPoints values per serving
14 ProPoints values per recipe

C **149 calories** per serving

Takes **15 minutes** to prepare,
10 minutes to cook

V

 not recommended

1 Sift the flour, baking powder and bicarbonate of soda into a bowl and add the salt and sugar. Cut the banana in half – roughly dice one half and thinly slice the other. Put to one side.

2 In a clean, grease-free bowl, whisk the egg white until stiff.

3 Put the low fat spread into a large jug and microwave for a few seconds on high until melted. Add the buttermilk, egg yolk and the diced half of the banana. Beat together to create a thick, fairly smooth mixture. Pour this into the dry ingredients and gently beat together to form a batter. Using a metal spoon, fold the egg white into the mixture.

4 Heat a flat griddle pan or non stick frying pan to a medium heat and spray with the cooking spray. When hot, use half of the batter to make four pancakes. They will be about 10 cm (4 inches) across. Cook the pancakes for 2–3 minutes on each side, turning them gently with a large palette knife. When cooked, remove and keep warm while you cook the other batch.

5 Serve immediately by placing two pancakes each on four warm plates. Scatter the banana slices over them and pour half a tablespoon of maple syrup over the top of each serving.

Bacon and Egg Frittata

Cooking in one pan is a wonderful easy way to cook brunch for several people, even saving on the washing up.

Serves 6

low fat cooking spray
1 onion, sliced thinly
4 lean back bacon rashers, cut into short strips
6 eggs
2 tablespoons chopped fresh parsley
350 g (12 oz) leftover cooked potatoes, sliced
salt and freshly ground black pepper

1 Heat a non stick frying pan, about 25 cm (10 inches) in diameter, and spray with the cooking spray. Gently sauté the onion for a couple of minutes then add the bacon and cook for another 2 minutes.

2 Meanwhile, beat the eggs in a large bowl with plenty of seasoning and the parsley. Add the onion, bacon and potatoes to the eggs and stir well.

3 Re-spray the pan with the cooking spray and heat until hot. Pour the egg mixture into the pan. Check that everything is evenly distributed, turn the heat down and leave to cook gently for 5 minutes. Meanwhile, preheat the grill to medium.

4 Put the pan under the grill for 5 minutes or until the eggs are completely set and the top is golden. Leave to cool in the pan for 10 minutes.

5 Remove the frittata by easing the edges with a palette knife or spatula and flipping it on to a plate. Cut into six slices. Serve cold for breakfast on the run (or a picnic lunch).

4 *ProPoints* values per serving
24 *ProPoints* values per recipe

C **167 calories** per serving

Takes **15 minutes**
+ **10 minutes** cooling

✱ not recommended

Tips If you prefer not to use the grill, you can carefully invert the frittata on to a plate after the initial cooking then slide it back into the pan to cook for 5 minutes on the other side.

If your frying pan has a plastic handle, cover it with foil before putting it under the grill to prevent it getting damaged.

Brunch

Everyone loves a cooked brunch, so treat yourself to this tasty dish.

Serves 2

205 g can baked beans
2 large field mushrooms,
   peeled
2 thick low fat sausages
4 bacon medallions

1 tomato, halved
low fat cooking spray
150 g (5½ oz) cooked new or
   small potatoes, sliced

1 Preheat the grill to high.

2 Put the baked beans in a small pan on a low heat to warm through
   (or you could microwave them in a suitable container).

3 Put the mushrooms and sausages under the grill and cook for
   5 minutes. Then add the bacon medallions and tomato halves and
   continue to cook for another 5 minutes or until everything is cooked
   to your taste.

4 Meanwhile, heat a non stick frying pan to a medium temperature and
   spray with the cooking spray. Sauté the sliced potatoes in the pan
   until golden brown – about 5 minutes.

5 Once everything is ready, share between two warmed plates and
   serve.

8 *ProPoints* values per serving
16 *ProPoints* values per recipe

C **167 calories** per serving

Takes **20 minutes**

＊ not recommended

Tip Can't have brunch without a fried egg? Fry an egg per person using
cooking spray, for 11 *ProPoints* values per serving.

Haddock Rarebit

This tasty fish dish is perfect for a light lunch or brunch.

Serves 2

2 x 200 g (7 oz) smoked haddock fillets
400 g (14 oz) frozen chopped spinach
75 g (2¾ oz) half fat Cheddar cheese, grated
2 tablespoons low fat mayonnaise
½ teaspoon mustard powder
1 teaspoon Worcestershire sauce
a shake of Tabasco sauce
½ teaspoon grated nutmeg
salt and freshly ground black pepper

9 *ProPoints* values per serving
17 *ProPoints* values per recipe

380 calories per serving

Takes **15 minutes** to prepare,
15 minutes to cook

* not recommended

1 Put the haddock fillets into a non stick frying pan and add 200 ml (7 fl oz) water. Poach gently for about 6–8 minutes until the fish is cooked; the flesh should be opaque and flake easily. Remove from the pan and set aside to cool.

2 Meanwhile, cook the spinach according to the packet instructions. Drain well and, when cool enough to handle, squeeze out any excess moisture. Transfer to two individual shallow, heatproof dishes. Season.

3 Remove the skin from the haddock then lay one fillet on top of the spinach in each dish. Preheat the grill to medium high.

4 Mix the cheese with the mayonnaise, mustard, Worcestershire sauce, Tabasco sauce and nutmeg. Spread this mixture over the fish fillets to cover them completely. Grill until browned and bubbling then serve at once.

Tip The dish can be finished off in the oven instead of under the grill. Simply bake for about 5–6 minutes at Gas Mark 6/200°C/fan oven 180°C.

Variation For a 'Buck Haddock Rarebit', add a poached egg and serve it on top of the fish and cheese, for 10 *ProPoints* values per serving.

Florentine Pizza

Placing the pizza dough in the oven for a short while helps it to rise more quickly and reduces the preparation time.

Serves 2

145 g packet pizza dough
300 g (10½ oz) spinach, rinsed
1 garlic clove, crushed
2 tablespoons tomato purée
2 eggs
salt and freshly ground black pepper

 8 ProPoints values per serving
16 ProPoints values per recipe

C **383 calories** per serving

⏲ Takes **15 minutes** to prepare,
15 minutes to cook

V

* not recommended

1 Preheat the oven to Gas Mark 7/220°C/fan oven 200°C.

2 Make up the dough according to the packet instructions, dividing it to make two pizzas. Roll out to circles of approximately 20 cm (8 inch) diameter and place on a baking tray (you may need two). Put in the oven for 2 minutes so that the dough begins to rise.

3 Cook the spinach in a steamer, or in a pan with 3 tablespoons of water, for 3–4 minutes until wilted. Drain well and, when cool enough to handle, squeeze out any excess water and chop roughly. Mix with the garlic and season.

4 Spread the tomato purée over the pizza bases and top with the spinach, making a well in the middle. Bake for 5 minutes then remove from the oven. Crack an egg into the middle of each pizza, so that it is contained within the spinach, and bake for a further 8–10 minutes until the bases are crispy.

Tip Eat hot, or cool it and then pack to enjoy for lunch.

Pineapple Lunch

Fruit, nuts and seafood may not seem like an obvious combination, but try this recipe for an unusual and tasty lunch.

Serves 4

1 ripe pineapple
225 g (8 oz) prawns, cooked and peeled
120 g (4½ oz) low fat natural yogurt
4 celery sticks, sliced thinly
20 cashew nuts
salt and freshly ground black pepper

---

3 *ProPoints* values per serving
10 *ProPoints* values per recipe

C 180 **calories** per serving

Takes **15 minutes**

✳ recommended

1 Cut the pineapple into quarters lengthways. Remove the flesh and dice it, leaving the shells intact. Set them aside.

2 In a large bowl carefully mix together the pineapple flesh and all the remaining ingredients. Season well. Spoon the salad back into the shells and serve. If you like, chill before serving.

Variation Try using the same amount of low fat mayonnaise instead of yogurt – the *ProPoints* values will be 5 per serving.

Lemon Chicken and Couscous Salad

This makes a great summer picnic dish.

Serves 4

250 g (9 oz) dried couscous
300 ml (10 fl oz) hot chicken stock
2 cm (¾ inch) fresh root ginger, peeled and grated
1 red pepper, de-seeded and halved
1 yellow pepper, de-seeded and halved
1 courgette, grated
1 small carrot, peeled and grated
1 tablespoon chopped fresh mint
2 tablespoons chopped fresh coriander
finely grated zest and juice of a lemon
2 cooked, skinless chicken breasts, shredded
salt and freshly ground black pepper
75 g (2¾ oz) watercress or salad leaves, to serve

---

8 *ProPoints* values per serving
33 *ProPoints* values per recipe

C **396 calories** per serving

Takes **20 minutes** + cooling

✱ recommended for up to 1 month

1 Preheat the grill to hot.

2 Place the couscous in a bowl and pour over the hot stock. Cover with a clean tea towel and leave to rest for 10–15 minutes. Add the grated ginger and stir around with a fork.

3 Meanwhile, place the halves of pepper, skin side up, under a hot grill and cook until very charred. Place in a bowl and cover with cling film until cool enough to handle. Peel off the skin and cut the flesh into strips.

4 When the couscous is cool, stir vigorously with a fork and then stir in all the other ingredients, including the peppers. Season well and serve on a bed of watercress or salad leaves.

Ham and Sweetcorn Pasta Lunchbox

Here's an ideal pasta salad for lunch that can be thrown together while you are cooking supper the night before.

Serves 4

150 g (5½ oz) dried conchigliette (mini pasta shells)
150 g (5½ oz) small broccoli florets
150 g (5½ oz) frozen sweetcorn
150 g (5½ oz) low fat natural cottage cheese
110 g (4 oz) smoked ham, diced
60 g (2 oz) Italian style salad leaves
salt and freshly ground black pepper
2 ripe tomatoes, sliced, to serve (optional)

---

6 ProPoints values per serving
26 ProPoints values per recipe

C **239 calories** per serving

Takes **15 minutes**

✱ not recommended

1 Bring a pan of water to the boil and cook the pasta for 5 minutes.

2 Add the broccoli florets and sweetcorn to the pasta and cook for a further 5 minutes. Drain and rinse in cold water.

3 Return to the pan. Toss the pasta and vegetables together with the cottage cheese and smoked ham, adding seasoning to taste. Divide between four lunchboxes. Top with the salad leaves but wait to mix them in until just before eating. Alternatively, toss in the salad leaves and serve on plates with tomato slices, if using.

Red Hot Prawn Pittas

Spicy prawns and delicious vegetables make this a quick and delicious lunch.

Serves 2

2 medium pitta breads
low fat cooking spray
½ red onion, sliced thinly
100 g (3½ oz) stir fry vegetables
½ red pepper, de-seeded and sliced thinly
75 g (2¾ oz) prawns, defrosted if frozen
1½ tablespoons sweet chilli sauce
salt and freshly ground black pepper

6 *ProPoints* values per serving
12 *ProPoints* values per recipe

C **250 calories** per serving

Takes **7 minutes**

✱ not recommended

1 Heat a wok or non stick frying pan until very hot. At the same time, warm the pitta breads in a toaster or under the grill.

2 Spray the wok or frying pan with the cooking spray then add the onion and stir fry for a few seconds.

3 Add the stir fry vegetables and red pepper and cook for another minute or two, stirring all the time.

4 Add the prawns and stir fry for another few moments to heat through. Stir in the chilli sauce, season, then stuff into the warmed pitta breads. Serve at once.

Variation Use the stir fry mixture to fill lightly toasted bagels or medium baked potatoes, remembering to add the *ProPoints* values.

For a vegetarian alternative, omit the prawns and use 75 g (2¾ oz) of drained canned chick peas instead. The *ProPoints* values will be 7 per serving.

Steak Sandwich with Onion Jam

Usually you have to pay a fortune for this sort of lunch in a flashy restaurant, but it is quick and easy and altogether more satisfying to take the trouble to make and eat at home.

Serves 2

1 French bread baton (about 150 g/5½ oz)
140 g (5 oz) beef steak
low fat cooking spray
2 red onions, sliced thinly
2 teaspoons caster sugar
2 teaspoons Dijon mustard
about 4–6 lettuce leaves
salt and freshly ground black pepper

10 ProPoints values per serving
20 ProPoints values per recipe

C **374 calories** per serving

Takes **25 minutes**

✱ not recommended

1 Halve the bread baton lengthways and then cut into two and place on two serving plates. Cut the steak in half and place both halves between two sheets of cling film or baking parchment. Beat with a rolling pin until thin, but be careful not to break up the meat.

2 Heat a non stick frying pan, spray with the cooking spray and fry the onions for about 5 minutes until softened. Sprinkle with the sugar and 2 tablespoons of water and continue to cook for about 5 minutes until all the water has evaporated and the onions have caramelised.

3 Remove the onions from the pan and set aside.

4 Season the steaks. Spray the pan with the cooking spray again and, when it is very hot, fry the steaks for 1 minute on each side.

5 Meanwhile, spread the bread with the mustard and top with some lettuce leaves. Place the cooked steaks on top and cover with onion jam. Replace the top halves and serve.

Variations Try with a 140 g (5 oz) grilled skinless chicken breast, prepared as step 1, instead of the steak, for 9 **ProPoints** values per serving.

Spicy Mango Chicken Pancakes

Serve these with a crisp green salad for no additional *ProPoints* values.

Makes 6 pancakes

127 g packet pancake batter mix
1 egg
low fat cooking spray
450 g jar curry cooking sauce
450 g (1 lb) cooked, skinless chicken breast, chopped
1 ripe mango, peeled, stoned and chopped
2 spring onions, chopped
3 firm tomatoes, sliced

---

5 *ProPoints* values per serving
31 *ProPoints* values per recipe

255 calories per serving

Takes **25 minutes**

* recommended

1 Make the pancake batter according to the packet instructions, adding the egg. Spray a small, non stick omelette or frying pan with the cooking spray and heat gently. Add a spoonful or two of batter to the pan, cook for 1–2 minutes until bubbles appear then turn over and cook until golden brown. Repeat to make six pancakes. Wrap the cooked pancakes in foil and keep warm under a low grill setting.

2 Gently heat the curry sauce in a pan and add the cooked chicken. Heat thoroughly, stirring, until piping hot.

3 Fold in the mango pieces and spring onion. Divide the filling between the pancakes. Fold into neat squares and arrange on a foil lined grill pan. Top each pancake with slices of tomato.

4 Heat through under the grill until the tomatoes are lightly cooked and the pancakes are hot.

Vegetable and Herb Salad with Toasted Bread (Fattoush)

This Lebanese recipe is a good way to use up stale bread, especially pitta bread.

Serves 4

2 medium pitta breads
8 Cos lettuce leaves, washed
½ cucumber, cut lengthways into quarters then diced
2 ripe tomatoes, diced
½ red or orange pepper, de-seeded and diced
a bunch of watercress, chopped roughly
a bunch of mint, chopped

For the dressing
juice of ½ a lemon
2 tablespoons low fat natural yogurt or virtually fat free fromage frais
1 tablespoon French or wholegrain mustard
salt and freshly ground black pepper

---

 3 ProPoints values per serving
 10 ProPoints values per recipe

C **155 calories** per serving

⊘ Takes **15 minutes**

V

✳ not recommended

1 Toast the pittas in the toaster or under the grill then cut into small squares.

2 Place two lettuce leaves on each serving plate. Put all the other salad ingredients, including the bread, into a large bowl.

3 Whisk together all the dressing ingredients. Pour over the salad and toss together. Spoon on to the lettuce leaves and serve.

Squid Salad

A deliciously fresh tasting salad.

Serves 4

850 ml (1½ pints) fish stock

300 g (10½ oz) fresh squid, sliced, keeping the tentacles whole

1 cucumber, cut in half lengthways, de-seeded then sliced thinly into half moons

1 tablespoon sesame seeds

100 g (3½ oz) Chinese leaves, chopped

salt and freshly ground black pepper

For the dressing

juice of a lime

1 teaspoon fish sauce

1 tablespoon soy sauce

1 fresh red chilli, de-seeded and chopped finely

2 spring onions, sliced

1 teaspoon caster sugar

2 tablespoons chopped fresh coriander

---

2 *ProPoints* values per serving
10 *ProPoints* values per recipe

C 125 calories per serving

Takes **20 minutes**

✱ not recommended

1 Whisk all the dressing ingredients together except for the coriander. Season.

2 In a medium saucepan, bring the stock to a gentle simmer and add the squid. Simmer for 3–4 minutes.

3 Drain the squid and put it into a bowl.

4 Add the coriander to the dressing and then pour it over the squid. Leave to cool slightly.

5 Add the cucumber slices, sesame seeds and Chinese leaves to the bowl and mix gently.

6 Check the seasoning and serve.

Turkey and Broccoli Pasta with Mustard Crème Fraîche

A filling and savoury lunch.

Serves 4

175 g (6 oz) dried pasta (e.g. fusilli, tagliatelle or spaghetti)
275 g (9½ oz) broccoli, broken into florets
low fat cooking spray
275 g (9½ oz) turkey breast strips
1 small onion, chopped
125 g (4½ oz) mushrooms, sliced
200 ml (7 fl oz) hot chicken stock
1 tablespoon Dijon mustard
2 teaspoons cornflour
4 tablespoons half fat crème fraîche
salt and freshly ground black pepper

8 *ProPoints* values per serving
32 *ProPoints* values per recipe

C   **310 calories** per serving

Takes **25 minutes**

✳   not recommended

1 Bring a large pan of water to the boil and cook the pasta for 10 minutes. Halfway through the cooking time add the broccoli to the pan.

2 Meanwhile, spray a large, non stick frying pan with the cooking spray, add the turkey, onion and mushrooms and cook for 3–4 minutes. Pour in the hot stock and bring to the boil. Blend the mustard and cornflour with the crème fraîche and stir this mixture into the frying pan. Simmer for 5 minutes.

3 Drain the pasta and broccoli thoroughly then combine them with the turkey and sauce. Season well. Divide between four warmed bowls and serve.

Variation Add a teaspoon of garlic purée to the turkey in step 2. The *ProPoints* values per serving will remain the same.

Mediterranean Vegetable and Pesto Filling

A versatile filling for sandwiches and wraps, this also makes a lovely topping for a jacket potato.

Serves 2

2 small courgettes, trimmed and sliced thinly, lengthways

½ red and ½ yellow pepper, de-seeded and sliced lengthways

4 spring onions, trimmed and each cut into 2 short sections

low fat cooking spray

1 tablespoon pesto sauce

60 g (2 oz) low fat soft cheese

2 medium slices wholemeal bread

---

5 ProPoints values per serving
9 ProPoints values per recipe

C **188 calories** per serving

🕐 Takes **20 minutes**

V

✱ not recommended

1 Preheat the grill to a high setting. Lightly coat all the vegetables with the cooking spray and spread them out on the grill tray. Grill the vegetables for about 4–5 minutes on each side, until tender and browned.

2 While the vegetables are cooking, mix the pesto into the soft cheese. To serve, spread the pesto mixture on to the slices of bread then top with the chargrilled vegetables.

Chilli Lamb Pittas

You can adjust the spiciness of this recipe to suit your palate by using more or less chilli powder. With a cooling cucumber and yogurt relish to temper the heat, these pittas are a great alternative to a kebab.

Serves 4

½ teaspoon ground cumin
¼ teaspoon chilli powder
300 g (10½ oz) lean lamb leg steaks
low fat cooking spray
50 g (1¾ oz) cucumber, diced
75 g (2¾ oz) low fat natural yogurt
4 medium pitta breads
75 g (2¾ oz) Iceberg lettuce, shredded
salt and freshly ground black pepper

8 ProPoints values per serving
32 ProPoints values per recipe

225 calories per serving

Takes **10 minutes**

✱ not recommended

1 Mix the cumin and chilli powder together with some seasoning then rub this spice mixture into the lamb steaks. Heat a non stick frying pan, spray with the cooking spray and pan fry the lamb steaks for 3–4 minutes on each side until cooked to your liking. Preheat the grill to medium.

2 Meanwhile, mix the cucumber into the yogurt to make the relish, and season to taste. Set aside.

3 Under a medium grill, lightly toast the pittas then cut each one in half to make two pockets. Stuff with shredded lettuce and spoon in the cucumber relish.

4 Slice the lamb into strips and pile into the pitta pockets. Serve immediately.

Beef Burritos

A burrito is a flour tortilla that has been folded and rolled to completely enclose a number of savoury fillings such as meat, re-fried beans, grated cheese, sour cream, lettuce and so on. Here, juicy strips of fillet steak and mushrooms provide a mouth-watering combination.

Serves 4

1½ teaspoons paprika
½ teaspoon ground cumin
a pinch of hot chilli powder
275 g (9½ oz) fillet steak, cut into thin strips
1 teaspoon sunflower oil
1 large onion, sliced
1 garlic clove, crushed
3 large flat mushrooms, sliced
215 g can re-fried beans
4 x 20 cm (8 inch) flour tortillas
4 tablespoons very low fat plain fromage frais
¼ Iceberg lettuce, shredded

8 ProPoints values per serving
33 ProPoints values per recipe

C **318 calories** per serving

Takes **20 minutes**

＊ not recommended

1 Mix the spices together and toss the strips of steak in the mixture. Set aside.

2 Heat the oil in a large, non stick frying pan, add the onion and stir fry for 3 minutes. Add the garlic and mushrooms and cook for 3 minutes until tender. Remove to a plate.

3 In the same pan, stir fry the steak strips for 3 minutes over a high heat then return the onion and mushrooms to the pan and toss everything together. Remove from the heat.

4 Heat the re-fried beans and the tortillas according to the packet instructions.

5 Spread each tortilla with a quarter of the re-fried beans then divide the steak mixture between them. Top with a tablespoon of fromage frais each and shredded lettuce. Roll up the tortillas, folding in the sides to enclose the filling. Serve straightaway.

Tip Very low fat plain fromage frais is a great low **ProPoints** value substitute for soured cream in Tex Mex recipes.

Variations Substitute 2 teaspoons Cajun seasoning for the individual spices if you prefer.

For vegetarian mushroom burritos, leave out the steak and use eight large flat mushrooms. The **ProPoints** values will be reduced to 6 per serving.

Chicken Livers on Toast

Chicken livers are tasty and take no time at all to cook. Adding some mushrooms, tomatoes and a slice of wholemeal toast makes a complete meal.

Serves 1

low fat cooking spray
50 g (1¾ oz) mushrooms, sliced
1 rasher smoked lean back bacon, chopped
1 garlic clove, crushed
150 g (5½ oz) whole chicken livers
1 tomato, chopped
1 medium slice wholemeal or granary bread

8 *ProPoints* values per serving
8 *ProPoints* values per recipe

C **238 calories** per serving

Takes **15 minutes**

* not recommended

1 Lightly spray a non stick frying pan with the cooking spray and heat until hot. Add the mushrooms and bacon and stir fry for 5 minutes until the bacon is beginning to brown.

2 Add the garlic and cook for a further minute. Add the chicken livers, tomato and 2 tablespoons of water. Reduce the heat and simmer for 3–4 minutes until the livers are tender.

3 Toast the slice of bread and serve the livers on top.

Tip For something more substantial, omit the toast and add 60 g (2 oz) of dried pasta, cooked according to packet instructions, into the mixture, for 12 *ProPoints* values.

Spanish Rice

Similar to the Spanish dish paella, this is deliciously satisfying.

Serves 4

250 g (9 oz) dried brown rice

400 g can chopped tomatoes with herbs

200 g (7 oz) cooked, skinless chicken breast, sliced

230 g packet mixed seafood (e.g. prawns, mussels, squid)

150 g (5½ oz) frozen peas

2 teaspoons smoked paprika (optional)

---

10 **ProPoints** values per serving
41 **ProPoints** values per recipe

368 calories per serving

Takes **10 minutes** to prepare,
10 minutes to cook

not recommended

1 Bring a pan of water to the boil and cook the rice according to the packet instructions. Drain well.

2 Place all the ingredients, including the rice, in a large, lidded, non stick frying pan and heat gently.

3 Add 1 tablespoon water, cover and simmer for 10 minutes until piping hot.

4 Serve in large bowls.

Tip Smoked paprika, or pimenton, adds a smoky flavour and is available in most larger supermarkets in the herbs and spice or exotic foods section.

Tzatziki Turkey Burgers

Turkey combined with added chilli and fresh coriander makes these burgers very tasty. Serve with crisp lettuce and tomatoes, for no additional *ProPoints* values.

Serves 4

low fat cooking spray
1 onion, chopped finely
2 garlic cloves, crushed
450 g (1 lb) turkey mince
1 small red chilli, de-seeded and chopped finely
a dash of Tabasco sauce
1 tablespoon soy sauce
a small bunch of fresh coriander, chopped
salt and freshly ground black pepper

For the sauce
½ cucumber, halved lengthways, de-seeded and diced finely
150 g (5½ oz) 0% fat Greek yogurt
a small handful of fresh mint, chopped

---

5 *ProPoints* values per serving
18 *ProPoints* values per recipe

C 185 **calories** per serving

Takes **20 minutes** to prepare,
10 minutes to cook

✳ recommended for uncooked burgers only

1 Spray a non stick frying pan with the cooking spray and fry the onion and garlic for about 5 minutes, until softened and golden, adding a little water if necessary to stop them sticking.

2 Place the turkey mince in a bowl and add the fried onion and garlic, chilli, Tabasco sauce, soy sauce, coriander and seasoning. Using your hands, shape into eight large patties. Preheat the grill and line the grill pan with foil.

3 Grill the burgers for about 5 minutes on each side or until cooked through and golden brown.

4 Meanwhile, make the sauce by mixing together the cucumber, Greek yogurt, mint and seasoning. Serve the burgers with the sauce.

American Beefburger

Juicy and full of flavour, this burger is made with prime extra lean beef to keep the **ProPoints** values as low as possible.

Serves 1

110 g (4 oz) extra lean beef mince
¼ small red onion, chopped very finely
1 small garlic clove, crushed
¼ teaspoon dried thyme
½ teaspoon dried oregano
a few drops of Tabasco sauce
1 egg white, beaten lightly
salt and freshly ground black pepper

To serve

50 g (1¾ oz) burger bun
shredded lettuce
1 tomato slice
1 dill pickle (large gherkin), sliced

---

8 ProPoints values per serving
8 ProPoints values per recipe

C **335 calories** per serving

Takes **10 minutes** to prepare,
15 minutes to cook

✳ not recommended

1 Preheat the grill and line the grill pan with foil. In a large bowl, mix all the burger ingredients together until thoroughly combined.

2 Using your hands, shape the mixture into a large burger.

3 Place the burger on the grill pan and cook for about 6–7 minutes on each side, until well browned.

4 To serve, place the burger in the bun and top with plenty of shredded lettuce, the tomato slice and the dill pickle.

Variation You could make this burger with lean lamb or turkey mince. The **ProPoints** values per serving will be 10 and 7 respectively.

Crab and Ginger Noodles

Crab and ginger go well together and this simple noodle dish is so easy to make.

Serves 4

250 g (9 oz) dried egg noodles

low fat cooking spray

a bunch of spring onions

2.5 cm (1 inch) fresh root ginger, peeled and cut into thin slivers

2 garlic cloves, sliced

1 red chilli, de-seeded and chopped finely (optional)

2 x 170 g cans crab meat

300 g (10½ oz) mange tout or sugarsnap peas

4 tablespoons soy sauce

1 packet fresh coriander, chopped

5 g (¼ oz) dry roasted peanuts, chopped to garnish

---

9 ProPoints values per serving
36 ProPoints values per recipe

350 calories per serving

Takes **5 minutes** to prepare,
10 minutes to cook

✳ not recommended

1 Bring a large pan of water to the boil and cook the noodles following the packet instructions. Drain, rinse and drain again. Set aside.

2 Spray a large, non stick frying pan or wok with the cooking spray and put on a high heat. Stir fry the spring onions, ginger, garlic and chilli, if using, for 1 minute.

3 Add the crab, mange tout or sugarsnap peas, noodles and soy sauce. Stir fry for 2 minutes.

4 Take the pan or wok off the heat, add the fresh coriander, divide between four plates and serve sprinkled with the peanuts.

Grapefruit and Beetroot Salad

This salad is lovely and refreshing when served on a warm summer's day.

Serves 2

1 grapefruit, segmented
25 g (1 oz) watercress
25 g (1 oz) baby spinach leaves
185 g (6½ oz) cooked beetroot, drained if
  necessary
1 teaspoon tahini
salt and freshly ground black pepper

0 *ProPoints* values per serving
1 *ProPoints* value per recipe

C **100 calories** per serving

Takes **10 minutes**

V

* not recommended

1 Mix the grapefruit and vegetables together in a salad bowl.

2 In a separate bowl, mix the tahini with 1 tablespoon of water. Pour this into the salad bowl.

3 Toss gently to coat all the ingredients with the tahini dressing, season and serve.

Light Bites
and Snacks

Fantastically flavoursome, these light bites and snacks are delicious too. Try Bombay Popcorn, Thai Beef Salad, Artichoke and Chicken Salad or Savoury Mini Muffins.

Give snacks a face lift with
these great healthy ideas

Prawn Pâté with Crispbreads

Ideal for a super quick meal. And it's so good you'll still feel like you're spoiling yourself.

Serves 4

300 g (10½ oz) peeled and cooked prawns
100 g (3½ oz) low fat natural cottage cheese
finely grated zest and juice of ½ a small lemon
a pinch of cayenne pepper
8 wholewheat crispbreads
75 g (2¾ oz) cucumber, sliced thinly
salt and freshly ground black pepper

4 ProPoints values per serving
16 ProPoints values per recipe

130 calories per serving

Takes **5 minutes**

not recommended

1 Reserve 50 g (1¾ oz) of the prawns to garnish, then place the rest of the prawns in a food processor with the cottage cheese, lemon zest and juice and cayenne pepper. Whizz to a thick paste. Season to taste.

2 Spread the pâté on to the crispbreads and top with the sliced cucumber and reserved prawns.

Garlic Mushrooms

Serve one mushroom each for a starter for two. For a light meal for one, accompany with steamed carrots, courgettes and broccoli instead of the lettuce and tomato, for 7 *ProPoints* values.

Serves 2

2 very large flat mushrooms, wiped
low fat cooking spray
2 spring onions, trimmed and chopped finely
125 g (4½ oz) low fat soft cheese with garlic and herbs
1 tablespoon fresh white breadcrumbs
1 tablespoon finely grated Parmesan cheese
salt and freshly ground black pepper
chopped fresh parsley, to garnish

To serve
shredded lettuce
cherry tomatoes

---

3 *ProPoints* values per serving
7 *ProPoints* values per recipe

115 calories per serving

Takes **10 minutes** to prepare,
15 minutes to cook

V

✳ not recommended

1 Preheat the oven to Gas Mark 6/200°C/fan oven 180°C.

2 Remove the stalks from the mushrooms and finely chop them. Spray a non stick frying pan with the cooking spray. Heat the pan, add the mushroom stalks and spring onions and cook them until softened – about 3 minutes. Cool slightly.

3 Meanwhile, spray each side of the mushroom caps with the cooking spray and put them in a baking dish with the brown gills facing upwards. Mix the soft cheese with the spring onion mixture and use it to fill the mushroom caps. Season.

4 Mix the breadcrumbs and Parmesan cheese together and sprinkle the mixture over the mushrooms. Bake for 10–12 minutes until cooked.

5 Garnish the mushrooms with chopped fresh parsley and serve with shredded lettuce and cherry tomatoes.

Tip If you can't find low fat soft cheese with garlic and herbs, just use the plain variety and add a crushed garlic clove to the frying pan with the spring onions. Stir a tablespoon of chopped fresh parsley – or herbs of your choice – into the mixture before filling the mushrooms. The *ProPoints* values will remain the same.

Spinach and Turkey Salad

A delicious salad that is full of flavour and colour.

Serves 4

4 medium slices bread, cubed
6 turkey rashers, cut crossways to make thin, short strips
225 g (8 oz) baby spinach leaves, washed and dried
12 cherry tomatoes

For the dressing
1 tablespoon balsamic vinegar
1 teaspoon French mustard
salt and freshly ground black pepper

1 Toast the bread cubes on a baking tray by placing them under the grill and toasting them on one side; then turn them over and toast again on the other side until golden all round.

2 Dry fry the turkey rasher strips in a non stick frying pan for 2 minutes, until golden.

3 Meanwhile, put the spinach and tomatoes into serving bowls. Sprinkle over the turkey strips and the croûtons.

4 Whisk the dressing ingredients and 2 tablespoons of water together in a bowl, pour over the salad and serve.

3 ProPoints values per serving
13 ProPoints values per recipe

145 calories per serving

Takes **10 minutes**

recommended

Bombay Popcorn

A fantastic and fun snack to enjoy in front of the telly.

Serves 4

1 teaspoon vegetable oil
75 g (2¾ oz) corn kernels
2 tablespoons soy sauce

1 teaspoon curry powder
salt and freshly ground black pepper

1 Heat the oil in a large, lidded saucepan until nearly smoking. Add the corn kernels and cover the pan with the lid. Shake vigorously from time to time over a medium high heat until you hear the corn starting to pop.

2 Shake the pan continuously until you no longer hear popping, then remove from the heat.

3 Shake over the soy sauce, curry powder and seasoning, then replace the lid and shake again until the popcorn is evenly coated. Tip into a large bowl and eat warm or cold.

3 ProPoints values per serving
12 ProPoints values per recipe

37 calories per serving

Takes **15 minutes**

V

✱ not recommended

Artichoke and Chicken Salad

Artichoke hearts provide a tasty twist for this delicious salad.

Serves 2

1 small red onion, cut into thin wedges
low fat cooking spray
4 baby courgettes, trimmed and halved
 lengthways
400 g can artichoke hearts in brine, drained and
 halved
1 tablespoon capers, rinsed well
2 tablespoons chopped fresh flat leaf parsley
25 g (1 oz) mild pepperdew peppers, drained and
 sliced finely
100 g (3½ oz) cooked, skinless chicken breast,
 sliced thinly
4 tablespoons balsamic vinegar
salt and freshly ground black pepper

2 *ProPoints* values per serving
4 *ProPoints* values per recipe

170 calories per serving

Takes **30 minutes**

not recommended

1 Put the onion in a bowl and spray with the cooking spray. Heat a griddle or non stick frying pan until hot and cook the onion wedges for 3 minutes. Put the courgettes and artichoke hearts in the bowl and spray with the cooking spray. Toss to coat.

2 Turn the onions over and add the courgettes and artichoke hearts. Cook for a further 5–8 minutes until chargrilled and tender, turning halfway.

3 Meanwhile, put the capers, parsley and peppers into a bowl. Add the chargrilled vegetables and gently toss to combine. Season. Divide the chicken slices between two plates and top each with half the warm chargrilled vegetables.

4 While the griddle or non stick frying pan is still warm, add the balsamic vinegar to deglaze the pan and bubble for a few seconds. Drizzle the sticky syrup over the vegetables and serve.

Variation For a vegetarian version, replace the cooked chicken with 60 g (2 oz) Quorn Deli Style wafer thin chicken in step 3, for 1 *ProPoints* value per serving.

Glazed Sausage Kebabs

A fun way to cook sausages and perfect for a light meal.

Makes 8

8 low fat sausages, each cut into thirds
2 courgettes, sliced thickly
8 small tomatoes, halved
2 dessert apples, cored and cut into eighths
4 small onions, quartered

For the glaze
2 tablespoons mango chutney
2 tablespoons orange juice
1 tablespoon wholegrain mustard
½ teaspoon ground ginger

1 Make the glaze by gently heating all the glaze ingredients together in a small pan, stirring to mix for a couple of minutes.

2 Meanwhile, heat the grill to medium. Thread alternate pieces of sausage, courgette, tomato, apple and onion on to eight small skewers.

3 Grill the kebabs for 12–15 minutes, brushing them with the glaze and turning them regularly. Mix any pan juices with leftover glaze and drizzle it over the kebabs to serve.

3 *ProPoints* values per serving
23 *ProPoints* values per recipe

140 calories per serving

Takes **10 minutes** to prepare,
15 minutes to cook

✳ not recommended

Crab Coleslaw

A tasty and light dish for when you are in a hurry.

Serves 4

2 x 170 g cans white crab meat in brine
½ red onion, sliced finely
1 apple, cored and sliced finely
150 g (5½ oz) white cabbage, cored and shredded finely
75 g (2¾ oz) cucumber, sliced finely
25 g packet fresh coriander, chopped roughly
1 small carrot, peeled and grated
1 avocado, peeled, stoned and sliced thinly

salt and freshly ground black pepper

For the dressing

finely grated zest and juice of 2 limes
4 tablespoons low fat plain fromage frais
1 teaspoon tomato purée
a few drops of Tabasco
½ teaspoon Worcestershire sauce

1 In a bowl, mix together all the dressing ingredients and season. Set aside. Drain one can of crab meat and empty into a large bowl. Mix in the onion, apple, cabbage, cucumber, coriander and carrot.

2 Add the dressing and toss gently to combine. Divide the avocado between four plates and top each with a generous amount of the crab coleslaw. Drain the remaining can of crab meat and crumble over the top of each salad.

4 *ProPoints* values per serving
17 *ProPoints* values per recipe

180 **calories** per serving

Takes **20 minutes**

not recommended

Thai Beef Salad

A brilliant way to use up the Sunday roast.

Serves 2

4 x 30 g (1¼ oz) slices of lean roast beef, shredded
1 teaspoon grated fresh root ginger
½ teaspoon Thai 7 spice blend
1½ tablespoons mature balsamic vinegar
2 spring onions, sliced finely
75 g (2¾ oz) radishes, trimmed and sliced finely
¼ cucumber, diced
2 large tomatoes, chopped
150 g (5½ oz) beansprouts

1 ProPoints value per serving
2 ProPoints values per recipe

161 calories per serving

Takes **10 minutes**

✱ not recommended

1 Mix together the beef, ginger, Thai 7 spice blend and balsamic vinegar in a large bowl.

2 Add the spring onions, radishes, cucumber, tomatoes and beansprouts.

3 Gently toss to mix. Divide between two plates and serve.

Cheesy Broccoli Soup

Broccoli not only has zero *ProPoints* values but is packed with flavour. It is especially delicious with cheese. This soup goes well with the Savoury Mini Muffins on page 82, for an extra 1 *ProPoints* value per serving.

Serves 2

300 g (10½ oz) broccoli, stalks included
150 g (5½ oz) potatoes, diced
600 ml (20 fl oz) vegetable stock
1 teaspoon dried thyme
40 g (1½ oz) Stilton cheese, crumbled, to serve

4 *ProPoints* values per serving
8 *ProPoints* values per recipe

197 calories per serving

Takes **5 minutes** to prepare,
15 minutes to cook

V

* recommended without the cheese

1 Chop the broccoli florets and stalks into bite sized pieces and place in a large, lidded pan with the potato, stock and thyme. Bring to the boil, cover and simmer for 15 minutes until the potato is tender.

2 Transfer to a liquidiser, or use a hand held blender, to blend the soup. Return to the pan to warm through, if necessary, and serve topped with the crumbled Stilton.

Tip Danish Blue is a great alternative to Stilton. It is quite salty though, so taste the soup first before seasoning it.

Onion Bhajis

Everybody loves these – and they're even better home made. Serve with the lovely fresh cucumber raita for a cooling contrast.

Serves 4

1 onion, sliced thinly
¼ teaspoon coriander seeds, crushed
¼ teaspoon cumin seeds
4 tablespoons plain flour
a pinch of salt
low fat cooking spray

For the raita

100 g (3½ oz) low fat natural yogurt
½ cucumber, grated
a bunch of fresh mint, chopped

 2 ProPoints values per serving
10 ProPoints values per recipe

C   **85 calories** per serving

⊘   Takes **10 minutes** to prepare,
20 minutes to cook

V

✱   not recommended

1   Place the onion, coriander and cumin seeds in a bowl and mix well. Sprinkle with the flour and salt. Mix again to coat the onion.

2   Add 2 tablespoons of water and mix until the onion is covered in a fine batter.

3   Heat a non stick frying pan and spray with the cooking spray. Place individual tablespoonfuls of the onion mixture in the pan and press down to flatten slightly. Cook on each side for about 4–5 minutes until golden. Keep the bhajis warm, either in the oven or under a moderate grill, while you cook the remaining mixture. The mixture will make about eight bhajis.

4   Mix together the ingredients for the raita and serve with the onion bhajis.

Garlic Prawns

One bite of these divine garlic prawns and your tastebuds will be transported to Spain, where they are served as a mouthwatering starter.

Serves 2

1 garlic clove, crushed
finely grated zest and juice of ½ a lemon
225 g (8 oz) cooked tiger prawns, with tails
1 teaspoon olive oil
1 tablespoon chopped fresh parsley
Maldon sea salt, or ordinary salt, and freshly ground black pepper
2 x 25 g (1 oz) slices of French bread, to serve

4 ProPoints values per serving
9 ProPoints values per recipe

215 calories per serving

Takes **10 minutes**
+ **15 minutes** marinating

✱ not recommended

1 Mix the garlic with the lemon zest and lemon juice in a shallow dish. Add the prawns and season with black pepper. Cover and leave to marinate for 15 minutes.

2 Heat a heavy based, non stick frying pan and add the prawns and their marinade. Cook over a high heat for 2–3 minutes, turning the prawns regularly.

3 Divide the prawns between two warm serving plates, drizzling any remaining juices over them. Sprinkle each portion with half a teaspoon of olive oil and a little parsley. Season with Maldon or ordinary salt according to taste and serve with the bread to mop up the juices.

Variation Replace the lemon half with a lime for a slightly sharper taste. Add a few drops of Tabasco sauce for a spicy flavour. The **ProPoints** values will remain the same.

Chicken and Apple Salad

A tasty, all-in-one meal, which is a variation on a traditional favourite.

Serves 4

100 g (3½ oz) low fat soft cheese

1 teaspoon Dijon mustard

6 tablespoons low fat natural yogurt

2 teaspoons lemon juice

200 g (7 oz) white cabbage, shredded finely

100 g (3½ oz) carrots, peeled and grated

¼ red onion, diced finely

250 g (9 oz) cooked, skinless chicken breasts, cut into chunks

1 apple, cored and sliced thinly

2 Little Gem lettuces, leaves separated

8 cherry tomatoes, halved

salt and freshly ground black pepper

4 parsley sprigs, to garnish (optional)

4 ProPoints values per serving
15 ProPoints values per recipe

203 calories per serving

Takes **15 minutes** to prepare

not recommended

1 Beat the soft cheese, mustard, yogurt and lemon juice together in a small bowl or jug. (A mini whisk is very useful to get a smooth consistency.)

2 Place the cabbage, carrots, onion, chicken and apple in a large mixing bowl and add the soft cheese mixture. Mix thoroughly and season to taste.

3 You can serve the salad immediately, or it will keep for at least 12 hours in a fridge. When ready to serve, place the lettuce leaves around the edges of four shallow bowls and put a quarter of the salad in the centre of each bowl. Serve topped with the halved tomatoes and if you're using parsley, sprinkle it over before serving.

Tip Use the soft cheese mixture as a dressing for other salads, instead of mayonnaise.

Variation This salad has a creamy taste. If you prefer a sharper flavour, increase the mustard and lemon juice a little.

Thai Chicken Noodle Soup

A familiar, soothing soup that is given a new twist with the addition of Thai curry spices and coconut milk.

Serves 4

low fat cooking spray
1 tablespoon Thai curry paste
2 onions, sliced thinly
2 garlic cloves, crushed
1 dried Kaffir lime leaf or the finely grated zest of a lime
2 litres (3½ pints) chicken stock
150 g (5½ oz) cooked, skinless chicken breast, shredded
125 g (4½ oz) dried rice noodles, broken into short lengths
100 ml (3½ fl oz) reduced fat coconut milk
a small bunch of fresh coriander or basil, chopped
salt and freshly ground black pepper
4 lime wedges, to serve (optional)

6 ProPoints values per serving
24 ProPoints values per recipe

205 calories per serving

Takes **15 minutes**

not recommended

1 Heat a large saucepan and spray with the cooking spray then add the curry paste and fry for 30 seconds. Add the onions, garlic and lime leaf or zest and a ladleful of chicken stock. Cook for 5 minutes until the onions are softened and the stock has evaporated.

2 Add the chicken and the remaining stock and bring to the boil. Add the noodles and simmer for 2–4 minutes. Remove from the heat, discard the lime leaf then stir in the coconut milk and coriander or basil and season to taste. Serve with the lime wedges, if using.

Tip Dried kaffir lime leaves are available in the spice sections of supermarkets.

Tabbouleh

This is a lovely summery, light salad, which originates in the Middle East and is traditionally served on a cos lettuce leaf, as a starter. Serve it with a Greek salad and remember to add the *ProPoints* values.

Serves 2

125 g (4½ oz) dried bulgur wheat
½ a kettleful of boiling water
2 spring onions, chopped
2 plum tomatoes, diced
¼ cucumber, diced
2 tablespoons chopped fresh mint
3 tablespoons chopped fresh parsley
juice of ½ a lemon
1 teaspoon wholegrain mustard
salt and freshly ground black pepper

5 *ProPoints* values per serving
10 *ProPoints* values per recipe

280 calories per serving

Takes **15 minutes**

V

＊ not recommended

1 Place the bulgur wheat in a bowl and pour over enough boiling water just to cover. Leave to soak for 15 minutes. Mix around with a fork to break up any lumps.

2 Mix in all the remaining ingredients and serve.

Cool Herby Chicken

This cool summery recipe is inspired by Greek salads found on the island of Crete.

Serves 6

150 g (5½ oz) 0% fat Greek yogurt

150 ml (5 fl oz) half fat crème fraîche

a small bunch of fresh coriander, chopped

a small bunch of fresh parsley, chopped

a small bunch of fresh mint, chopped

6 spring onions, sliced finely

2 x 125 g (4½ oz) cooked, skinless chicken breasts, cut into bite size pieces

1½ teaspoons ground coriander

1½ teaspoons ground cumin

salt and freshly ground black pepper

a few sprigs of fresh coriander, mint and parsley, to garnish

To serve

crisp green salad leaves

cherry tomatoes, halved

cucumber, sliced

---

3 ProPoints values per serving
17 ProPoints values per recipe

125 calories per serving

Takes **10–15 minutes**

＊ not recommended

1 Combine all the ingredients except the garnish and serving ingredients in a large bowl. Leave to stand for at least 5 minutes to allow time for the flavours to develop.

2 Spoon the mixture on to serving plates, garnish with sprigs of fresh herbs. Serve with a crisp green salad, tomatoes and cucumber.

Variation Try using chopped cucumber instead of chicken for a delicious vegetarian alternative.

Vegetable Spring Rolls with Sweet Chilli Sauce

A pack of ready prepared stir fry vegetables makes light work for these crispy little spring rolls.

Serves 4

low fat cooking spray
300 g (10½ oz) stir fry vegetables
1 teaspoon grated fresh root ginger
2 garlic cloves, crushed
¼ teaspoon Chinese five spice
1 tablespoon soy sauce
110 g (4 oz) water chestnuts, drained and sliced
4 x 45 g (1½ oz) sheets filo pastry
2 teaspoons sunflower oil
1 teaspoon sesame oil

For the sauce

1 tablespoon soy sauce
3 tablespoons sweet chilli sauce
juice of ½ a lime

5 ProPoints values per serving
21 ProPoints values per recipe

166 calories per serving

Takes **10 minutes** to prepare,
15 minutes to cook

V

 recommended

1 Heat a wok or large, non stick frying pan. Lightly coat with the cooking spray then stir fry the vegetables, ginger, garlic and Chinese five spice for 2 minutes. Add the soy sauce and water chestnuts and remove the pan from the heat. Leave to cool slightly.

2 Preheat the oven to Gas Mark 6/200°C/fan oven 180°C.

3 Cut each sheet of filo in half widthways. Stack the pieces of filo together and keep them covered with a clean damp tea towel while you work.

4 Mix the sunflower oil and sesame oil together in a small bowl. Take a piece of filo and brush lightly with the blended oil. Fold it in half to give a long narrow rectangle then place a spoonful of vegetables at one end. Roll up the pastry, folding in the sides to hold in the filling. Place on a non stick baking tray. Repeat with the rest of the filo sheets and filling to make eight spring rolls, then brush the rolls with any remaining oil.

5 Bake for 13–15 minutes until crisp and golden.

6 Mix the sauce ingredients together and serve with the spring rolls.

Chicory and Ham Salad

Chicory leaves are very crisp and have a pleasant, slightly bitter flavour that perfectly complements the ham and cheese in this salad.

Serves 4

4 heads of chicory, broken into separate leaves
10 cm (4 inch) piece of cucumber, chopped
a bunch of radishes, trimmed and halved
175 g (6 oz) lean cooked ham, cut into small cubes
50 g (1¾ oz) Edam cheese, cut into small cubes

For the dressing

150 g (5½ oz) low fat natural yogurt
1 teaspoon finely grated orange or lemon zest
1 tablespoon chopped fresh parsley or chives
salt and freshly ground black pepper

3 *ProPoints* values per serving
11 *ProPoints* values per recipe

155 **calories** per serving

Takes **10 minutes**

not recommended

1 Arrange the chicory leaves on four serving plates.

2 In a mixing bowl, combine the cucumber, radishes, ham and cheese. Spoon an equal amount on to each plate.

3 Mix together the yogurt, orange or lemon zest and parsley or chives. Add a little seasoning then spoon over the salads.

Chinese Style Scrambled Eggs

Serve this tasty snack on toast; a medium slice of wholemeal bread per person will add 2 *ProPoints* values per serving.

Serves 2

1 teaspoon sunflower oil
4 spring onions, sliced
100 g (3½ oz) fresh beansprouts
3 eggs
3 tablespoons skimmed milk
1 tablespoon light soy sauce
50 g (1¾ oz) cooked prawns, peeled

4 *ProPoints* values per serving
8 *ProPoints* values per recipe

215 **calories** per serving

Takes **15 minutes**

not recommended

1 Heat the sunflower oil in a small, non stick frying pan and add the spring onions and beansprouts. Stir fry for 2 minutes until they begin to soften.

2 Beat together the eggs, milk and soy sauce, and add the mixture to the pan with the prawns. Cook, stirring continuously, until the eggs begin to scramble. This will take about 5 minutes. Serve immediately.

Calamari Rings with Spicy Salsa

Why deep fry squid rings when you can increase the taste and lower the *ProPoints* values with this easy adaptation.

Serves 4

350 g (12 oz) squid rings
2 tablespoons skimmed milk
50 g (1¾ oz) dried polenta or instant semolina
low fat cooking spray
salt and freshly ground black pepper

For the salsa

2 large tomatoes, chopped finely
1 small red onion, chopped finely
¼ cucumber, chopped finely
2 tablespoons tomato ketchup
2 tablespoons fresh coriander or parsley, chopped
a pinch of dried chilli flakes or chilli powder

3 *ProPoints* values per serving
14 *ProPoints* values per recipe

153 **calories** per serving

Takes **20 minutes** to prepare,
10 minutes to cook

not recommended

1 First make the salsa by mixing together all the salsa ingredients. Season and set aside.

2 Pat the squid rings dry with kitchen towel, then put them into a bowl with the milk. Season.

3 Put the polenta or semolina into a large polythene bag or sprinkle it on to a plate. Add the squid rings and toss to coat.

4 Spray a large, non stick frying pan with the cooking spray. Add a few squid rings and cook for 4–6 minutes, turning once. Cook the rest in batches, spraying the pan each time with the cooking spray. Drain on kitchen towel. Serve with the salsa.

Tip Be careful not to overcook the squid as it can turn rubbery.

Polenta Slice

In this delicious recipe, polenta is served like a frittata or large omelette. Serve each with a portion of mixed leaves and a squeeze of lemon juice for no additional *ProPoints* values per serving.

Serves 4

20 g (¾ oz) sun-dried tomatoes
½ a kettleful of boiling water
low fat cooking spray
2 red peppers, de-seeded and sliced
1 large red onion, sliced
6 fresh sage leaves, shredded
800 ml (1 pint 7 fl oz) vegetable stock
200 g (7 oz) dried polenta
60 g (2 oz) half fat mature Cheddar cheese, grated
freshly ground black pepper

6 *ProPoints* values per serving
26 *ProPoints* values per recipe

275 calories per serving

Takes **10 minutes** to prepare + soaking, **12 minutes** to cook

V

✳ not recommended

1 Place the sun-dried tomatoes in a small bowl, cover with 150 ml (5 fl oz) of boiling water and soak for 10 minutes. Drain and chop.

2 Meanwhile, spray a grill-proof frying pan with the cooking spray and heat until hot. Add the peppers and onions and cook for 5 minutes, adding a little water if they begin to stick. Stir in the sage and remove from the heat.

3 In a medium, non stick pan, bring the stock to the boil and add the polenta quickly. Stir continuously for 2–3 minutes until thick and stiff. Stir in the vegetables, tomatoes and half the cheese. Season with some black pepper to taste, the stock should make it salty enough.

4 Preheat the grill to medium. Re-spray the frying pan with the cooking spray and heat until hot. Add the polenta mixture, pressing it down to fit. Cook for 3–4 minutes until firm. Remove from the heat, scatter over the remaining cheese and grill until bubbling. Serve in wedges.

Tips If your frying pan isn't grill proof, loosen the polenta from the pan and slide on to a baking tray before grilling the top.

Polenta needs plenty of strong flavours to make it tasty – robust herbs such as rosemary, sage and chives are useful as well as chilli, citrus zest, strong flavoured cheeses and garlic.

Spiced Beef Kebabs

Serve these mildly spiced beef kebabs on a bed of crisp zero *ProPoints* value mixed salad, accompanied by 1 tablespoon of low fat natural yogurt per person, for an extra *ProPoints* value of 1 per serving.

Serves 2

juice of a small lemon
1 teaspoon medium curry powder
¼ teaspoon dried mint
250 g (9 oz) rump steak, trimmed and cut into 2.5 cm (1 inch) cubes
1 red onion, chopped roughly
1 red pepper, de-seeded and chopped roughly
salt and freshly ground black pepper

6 *ProPoints* values per serving
11 *ProPoints* values per recipe

204 calories per serving

Takes **10 minutes** to prepare, **8–10 mintes** to cook

* not recommended

1 Preheat the grill to its highest setting.

2 Mix the lemon juice, curry powder, mint and seasoning together in a bowl. Stir in the diced steak, red onion and pepper and mix well to coat in the spice mixture.

3 Thread the cubes of spiced beef on to skewers, alternating with pepper and red onion. Grill for 8–10 minutes, turning once or twice, until cooked to your liking.

Minestrone Verde

This soup is packed with flavour and makes a refreshing lunch.

Serves 4

low fat cooking spray
2 rashers unsmoked, lean back bacon, rinds removed and chopped
2 onions, chopped
2 garlic cloves, crushed
2 celery sticks, sliced thinly
1.2 litres (2 pints) vegetable stock
50 g (1¾ oz) small dried pasta shapes
300 g can borlotti beans, rinsed and drained
200 g (7 oz) green beans, diced
200 g (7 oz) courgettes, diced finely
100 g (3½ oz) frozen petit pois
salt and freshly ground black pepper

To serve

fresh basil, chopped roughly (optional)
4 teaspoons pesto sauce

4 **ProPoints** values per serving
18 **ProPoints** values per recipe

195 **calories** per serving

Takes **5 minutes** to prepare,
20 minutes to cook

* recommended

1 Heat a large, non stick pan and spray with the cooking spray. Fry the bacon over a high heat until crispy. Reduce the heat, add the onions, garlic and celery and cook for 5 minutes until softened, stirring gently.

2 Pour the stock over and bring to the boil. Add the pasta and cook for 10 minutes then add the vegetables and cook for a further 5 minutes or until the pasta is cooked. Finally, check the seasoning, scatter the basil over, if using, and serve with a swirl of pesto sauce on top of each serving.

Variation You could use a 500 g bag of frozen mixed vegetables instead of all the fresh vegetables for a quick alternative.

Baby Herb and Cheese Scones

These little tasty scones go well with so many things. Add them to soups or salads to make a filling meal.

Makes 26

225 g (8 oz) self raising flour, plus 1 tablespoon for dusting
¼ teaspoon salt
40 g (1½ oz) low fat spread
1 teaspoon dried herbs (e.g. oregano, marjoram or mixed herbs)
50 g (1¾ oz) half fat mature Cheddar cheese, grated
½ teaspoon mustard powder
150 ml (5 fl oz) skimmed milk

1 *ProPoints* value per serving
30 *ProPoints* values per recipe

47 calories per serving

Takes **15 minutes** to prepare,
15 minutes to bake

V

✱ not recommended

1 Preheat the oven to Gas Mark 7/220°C/fan oven 200°C. Line a baking tray with baking parchment.

2 Sieve the flour into a large bowl and mix in the salt. Add the low fat spread and rub with your fingertips until the mixture resembles breadcrumbs. Stir in the herbs, cheese and mustard.

3 Make a well in the centre and gradually stir in all but 2 tablespoons of the milk. Turn out on to a floured surface. Knead quickly and lightly until smooth.

4 Press out the dough gently, with the palms of your hands, to about 1 cm (½ inch) thick. Cut into rounds about 3 cm (1¼ inches) in diameter. Place on the prepared baking tray. Press together the trimmings and repeat the rolling and cutting process until the dough is used up.

5 Brush the scones with the reserved milk and bake for 12–15 minutes, until risen and golden. Cool on a rack.

Savoury Mini Muffins

These mini muffins make a great alternative to bread. Try them with soup, salad or on their own as a tasty snack.

Makes 16

150 g (5½ oz) self raising flour
1 teaspoon baking powder
2 teaspoons chopped fresh thyme
4 x 15 g (½ oz) sun-dried tomatoes, reconstituted according to the packet instructions
1 egg
1 egg white
40 g (1½ oz) low fat spread, melted
low fat cooking spray (if needed)
salt and freshly ground black pepper

1 ProPoints value per serving
22 ProPoints values per recipe

51 calories per serving

Takes **20 minutes**

V

✳ recommended

1 Preheat the oven to Gas Mark 6/200°C/fan oven 180°C. If you don't have a non stick muffin tin, lay 16 paper cases on a baking tray.

2 Sift the flour and baking powder into a large bowl. Stir in the thyme and season. Drain the tomatoes, reserving 3 tablespoons of the soaking liquid, and dry them. Cut into small pieces and stir into the flour.

3 Beat together the egg and egg white. Add the low fat spread and reserved soaking liquid and then add this to the flour mix quickly. Do not beat. If using, spray the muffin tin with the cooking spray. Spoon the mixture into the tin or into the paper cases. Bake for 8–10 minutes until risen and golden. Serve warm or cold.

Tip The muffins are best if eaten the same day, but you could freeze them and warm through in the oven once defrosted. Alternatively, they can be stored in an airtight container for up to 2 days.

Easy
Suppers

Create a lovely meal at the end of day with very little effort. Try Steak and Shallots in Red Wine, Summer Vegetable Fusilli, Mussels with Tarragon or Vietnamese Beef and Noodle Stir Fry.

Delight family and friends with these great supper dishes

Spiced Lamb Steaks with Couscous

Cumin is a classic Middle Eastern spice that goes particularly well with lamb.

Serves 2

finely grated zest and juice of ½ a lemon
1 red chilli, de-seeded and diced
1 teaspoon cumin seeds
2 x 150 g (5½ oz) lean lamb leg steaks
low fat cooking spray
100 g (3½ oz) dried couscous
½ a kettleful of boiling water
2 tablespoons fresh coriander, chopped
salt and freshly ground black pepper

---

12 *ProPoints* values per serving
25 *ProPoints* values per recipe

C 288 **calories** per serving

Takes **4 minutes** to prepare,
8 minutes to cook

✱ not recommended

1 On a plate, mix together the lemon zest, half the chilli, cumin seeds and seasoning. Press the lamb steaks into the mixture to coat the meat.

2 Lightly coat a non stick frying pan with the cooking spray and fry the lamb steaks for 3–4 minutes on each side, until done to your liking.

3 Meanwhile, mix the lemon juice and remaining chilli into the couscous in a bowl. Season and add 175 ml (6 fl oz) of boiling water. Stir the mixture then cover the bowl with cling film and leave the couscous to stand for 5 minutes to soften.

4 Fluff up the couscous with a fork and mix in the coriander. Serve the lamb steaks on a bed of couscous.

Summer Vegetable Fusilli

This vibrant pasta dish has a wonderfully fresh flavour, with a touch of creamy richness from the half fat crème fraîche. Serve with a large mixed zero *ProPoints* value salad.

Serves 4

300 g (10½ oz) dried fusilli
150 g (5½ oz) green beans, halved
150 g (5½ oz) mange tout
low fat cooking spray
2 courgettes, diced
2 garlic cloves, crushed
zest of a lemon, plus 1 tablespoon juice
4 tablespoons half fat crème fraîche
4 heaped tablespoons chopped fresh basil
salt and freshly ground black pepper

9 *ProPoints* values per serving
35 *ProPoints* values per recipe

335 calories per serving

Takes **20 minutes**

V

✳ not recommended

1 Bring a large pan of water to the boil and cook the fusilli for 7 minutes.

2 Add the green beans and cook for a further 3 minutes, then add the mange tout and cook for 2 minutes more, or until the fusilli is tender.

3 While the pasta is cooking, heat a lidded, non stick pan, spray with the cooking spray and fry the courgettes for 3–4 minutes until lightly browned. Stir in the garlic and 2 tablespoons of water and season. Reduce the heat, cover and cook for 3 minutes or until tender.

4 Drain the pasta and vegetables, reserving 4 tablespoons of the cooking water. Return to the pan and stir in the courgettes, lemon zest and juice, crème fraîche and basil, plus the reserved cooking water. Season well and serve in warmed bowls.

Pad Thai

Stir fries are so quick to make – especially if you use ready prepared fresh vegetables.

Serves 4

200 g (7 oz) dried rice noodles
low fat cooking spray
2 teaspoons Thai 7 spice paste
150 g (5½ oz) cooked, shelled tiger prawns
**500 g (1 lb 2 oz) zero *ProPoints* value green
   vegetables (e.g. pak choi, Chinese leaves,
   watercress, spinach, broccoli, mange tout,
   green beans, beansprouts)**
2 tablespoons soy sauce

To garnish
a small bunch of fresh coriander, chopped
25 g (1 oz) dry roasted peanuts, chopped

7 *ProPoints* values per serving
29 *ProPoints* values per recipe

285 calories per serving

Takes **30 minutes**

✳ not recommended

1 Bring a large pan of water to the boil and then take off the heat. Add the rice noodles and leave to soak as directed on the packet or until just tender. Drain and refresh under cold water but reserve a little of the soaking water. Place the noodles in a bowl and snip with scissors to make shorter lengths.

2 Heat a large, non stick frying pan or wok and spray with the cooking spray. Add the spice paste and stir fry for about 30 seconds until it becomes fragrant then add the prawns and stir fry for 2 minutes.

3 Add the vegetables and soy sauce and stir fry together, with a few tablespoons of the reserved noodle soaking water, until the vegetables are tender.

4 Add the noodles to the mixture, toss together and heat through. Serve garnished with the coriander and peanuts.

Chicken and Mushroom Risotto

Choose Italian arborio rice and freshly grated Parmesan cheese to make the best risotto; flavour is everything when you're watching your weight.

Serves 4

2 tablespoons olive oil
225 g (8 oz) dried risotto rice
225 g (8 oz) skinless boneless chicken breasts, chopped into chunks
2 garlic cloves, crushed
1 onion, chopped
1 yellow or green pepper, de-seeded and sliced
100 g (3½ oz) mushrooms, wiped and sliced
2 teaspoons dried mixed Italian herbs
1 litre (1¾ pints) chicken or vegetable stock
25 g (1 oz) sun-dried tomatoes in olive oil, rinsed and sliced
salt and freshly ground black pepper

To serve
4 tablespoons freshly grated Parmesan cheese
a few sprigs of fresh basil

---

11 *ProPoints* values per serving
43 *ProPoints* values per recipe

415 calories per serving

Takes **10 minutes** to prepare,
20 minutes to cook

✱ recommended

1 Heat the oil in a large, lidded frying pan or wok. Add the rice and cook gently for 2 minutes. Add the chunks of chicken and cook for a further 2–3 minutes, stirring constantly.

2 Add the garlic, onion and pepper. Cook over a low heat, stirring frequently, for 5 minutes. Add the mushrooms and cook for another minute or so.

3 Stir in the dried herbs, half the stock and the sun-dried tomatoes. Bring to the boil, then reduce the heat. Cover and simmer gently for about 20 minutes, adding further stock as needed, until the rice is tender and all the stock has been absorbed.

4 Season the risotto, then ladle on to warmed plates and sprinkle each portion with 1 tablespoon of Parmesan cheese. Garnish with sprigs of fresh basil.

Tip If all the stock has been absorbed before the rice is tender, add a little more stock or hot water.

Variation You could add 2 skinned and chopped fresh tomatoes in step 3, just 5 minutes before the end of the cooking time. The *ProPoints* values will remain the same.

Steak and Shallots in Red Wine

Serve this with a zero *ProPoints* value green vegetable such as green beans.

Serves 2

8 shallots, peeled and quartered
low fat cooking spray
2 x 150 g (5½ oz) sirloin steaks, visible fat removed
4 tablespoons balsamic vinegar
150 ml (5 fl oz) red wine
150 ml (5 fl oz) beef or vegetable stock
salt and freshly ground black pepper

---

7 *ProPoints* values per serving
15 *ProPoints* values per recipe

293 calories per serving

Takes **5 minutes** to prepare,
20 minutes to cook

* not recommended

1 Simmer the shallots in a pan of boiling water for 2–3 minutes, drain and set aside.

2 Spray a non stick frying pan with the cooking spray, season the steaks and fry for 3–4 minutes on each side, or until cooked to your liking.

3 Remove the steaks to a plate and keep warm. Add the shallots to the pan and stir fry until browned. Add the balsamic vinegar and allow to bubble while you scrape up all the stuck on bits.

4 Add the wine and boil until the sauce is sticky. Add the stock and simmer for a few minutes until thickened.

5 Spoon the shallots and sauce over the steaks and serve immediately.

Variation For a vegetarian version, use large portabello mushrooms, 1 or 2 per person, in place of the steak, and vegetable stock, for 2 *ProPoints* values per serving.

Salmon and Dill Fish Pie

A tomato-based fish pie with sweet, fresh dill and succulent salmon. Serve with a crisp green salad for no extra *ProPoints* values.

Serves 4

750 g (1 lb 10 oz) potatoes, peeled and chopped
325 g (11½ oz) salmon fillets
150 ml (5 fl oz) skimmed milk
low fat cooking spray
175 g (6 oz) mushrooms, chopped
2 celery sticks, diced
100 g (3½ oz) fresh spinach, rinsed
6 tablespoons low fat fromage frais
3 tablespoons chopped fresh dill
salt and freshly ground black pepper

1 Preheat the oven to Gas Mark 6/200°C/fan oven 180°C.

2 Bring a pan of water to the boil and cook the potatoes until tender.

3 Meanwhile, place the salmon and milk in a small pan and simmer for 4–5 minutes until the salmon is just cooked. Drain, reserving the milk. Flake the salmon into big chunks.

4 Heat a large, lidded pan and spray with the cooking spray. Add the mushrooms and celery and cook for 4–5 minutes. Stir in the spinach, cover and cook for another 2–3 minutes until the spinach has wilted.

5 Add the salmon and fromage frais, stir well to combine and simmer for 1–2 minutes before stirring in the dill and seasoning. Pour into a shallow dish.

6 Drain the potatoes and mash with 100 ml (3½ fl oz) of the milk that was used to cook the salmon. Season well and spoon over the salmon.

7 Place in the oven and cook for 10 minutes until the potato topping is bubbling and golden.

9 *ProPoints* values per serving
36 *ProPoints* values per recipe

C **324 calories** per serving

Takes **15 minutes** to prepare, **10 minutes** to cook

* recommended for filling for up to 1 month

Chicken and Ricotta Parcels

You will need some cocktail sticks for this recipe.

Serves 4

100 g (3½ oz) ricotta cheese
2 sprigs of fresh rosemary or
   sage, chopped, or 1 teaspoon
   dried rosemary or sage
1 shallot, chopped finely
4 x 150 g (5½ oz) skinless
   boneless chicken breasts

350 g (12 oz) dried ribbon
   pasta
2 tablespoons honey
1 teaspoon chilli powder or
   cayenne pepper
salt and freshly ground black
   pepper

1 In a bowl, mix the ricotta cheese with the chopped herbs, shallot and seasoning. Cut a deep slit in the side of the chicken breast and open out to form a pocket. Stuff each breast with a spoonful of the cheese mixture. Secure the pocket with a cocktail stick. Preheat the grill to high.

2 Bring a pan of water to the boil and cook the pasta according to the packet instructions. Drain.

3 Meanwhile, in a small pan, mix the honey and chilli powder or cayenne pepper and heat gently. Brush the chicken with the honey mixture and place under the hot grill for 7–8 minutes or until cooked through. Remove the cocktail sticks before serving the chicken with the pasta.

14 *ProPoints* values per serving
56 *ProPoints* values per recipe

C **509 calories** per serving

Takes **10 minutes** to prepare,
15 minutes to cook

✱ not recommended

Pasta Arrabiatta

This is a fast and fabulous version of the classic Italian recipe.

Serves 2

low fat cooking spray

2 rashers smoked lean back bacon, trimmed of excess fat and chopped into strips

1 large garlic clove, chopped

½–1 teaspoon dried chilli flakes

400 g can chopped tomatoes with herbs

150 g (5½ oz) dried pasta shapes or spaghetti

salt and freshly ground black pepper

1 tablespoon chopped fresh parsley, to serve

---

9 ProPoints values per serving
18 ProPoints values per recipe

C **338 calories** per serving

Takes **5 minutes** to prepare,
15 minutes to cook

* recommended

1 Heat a medium, non stick pan until you can feel a good heat rising and spray with the cooking spray. Add the bacon and cook on a medium heat for 2 minutes.

2 Add the garlic and enough chilli flakes to suit your taste and then cook for a further 2 minutes. Stir in the tomatoes and seasoning and cook for 10 minutes, stirring once or twice.

3 Meanwhile, bring a pan of water to the boil and cook the pasta for about 8 minutes or according to the packet instructions. Drain and then mix in the tomato and chilli sauce. Serve the pasta sprinkled with the parsley.

Fillet Steak Tournedos

Serve with some baby leaks or some steamed baby carrots and 100 g (3½ oz) boiled potatoes per person, for an extra 2 *ProPoints* values per serving.

Serves 2

250 g (9 oz) fillet steak, halved vertically
low fat cooking spray
2 thin slices (2.5 cm/1 inch) French bread

For the garlic butter

1 tablespoon finely chopped fresh flat leaf
** parsley**
1 tablespoon half fat butter
1 garlic clove, crushed
salt and freshly ground black pepper

7 *ProPoints* values per serving
14 *ProPoints* values per recipe

290 calories per serving

Takes **15 minutes**

＊ not recommended

1 Make the garlic butter by mashing together the parsley, butter and garlic and season well. Form into a sausage shape and roll in cling film. Put in the freezer to chill.

2 Preheat the grill to high. Spray the steaks with the cooking spray.

3 For medium steaks, grill the steaks for 5 minutes on each side. For well-done steaks, cook a little longer.

4 Meanwhile, toast the bread.

5 When the steaks are cooked to your liking, place on the toast and top with slices of the chilled butter.

Lamb Jalfrezi

This dish is a very popular choice on restaurant menus throughout Great Britain and this version is delicious. Serve with 60 g (2 oz) cooked basmati rice per person, for an extra 6 **ProPoints** values per serving.

Serves 4

low fat cooking spray
500 g (1 lb 2 oz) lean lamb leg steaks, cut into strips
1 large onion, sliced
1 red pepper, de-seeded and sliced
1 green pepper, de-seeded and sliced
2 tablespoons Madras curry paste
400 g can chopped tomatoes
2 tablespoons tomato purée
100 g (3½ oz) low fat natural yogurt

1 Place a large, non stick frying pan on the hob to heat. Spray with the cooking spray and fry the lamb until lightly browned. Remove it to a plate.

2 Add the onion and peppers and brown for 5 minutes, then return the meat to the pan. Stir in the curry paste and fry for 30 seconds before adding the tomatoes and tomato purée. Stir in 150 ml (5 fl oz) of hot water, bring to the boil and simmer for 10 minutes until the meat and vegetables are tender. Remove from the heat, stir in the yogurt and serve.

8 **ProPoints** values per serving
33 **ProPoints** values per recipe

C **264 calories** per serving

Takes **15 minutes** to prepare, **10 minutes** to cook

✳ recommended

Seared Salmon with Tangy Avocado Salsa

Serve with 100 g (3½ oz) boiled new potatoes per person for an extra 2 **ProPoints** values per serving.

Serves 4

4 x 125 g (4½ oz) skinless salmon fillets
low fat cooking spray
salt and freshly ground black pepper

For the salsa

1 avocado, peeled, stoned and diced
100 g (3½ oz) cherry tomatoes, diced
finely grated zest and juice of ½ a lime
2 tablespoons fresh coriander, chopped

1 Preheat a non stick frying pan on the hob.

2 Lightly spray the salmon fillets with the cooking spray and season. Cook for 2–3 minutes on each side, or until cooked to your liking.

3 While the salmon is cooking, mix the salsa ingredients together and season. Serve the salsa spooned over the salmon.

  8 ProPoints values per serving
  32 ProPoints values per recipe

C **300 calories** per serving

Takes **10 minutes**

* not recommended

Tip To prepare an avocado, cut in half then run a dessertspoon between the skin and the flesh to release it easily in one piece. Remove the stone and dice or slice as required.

Orange Mustard Chicken with Parsnip Mash

An unusual dish, this sounds fancy but is quick and easy. A perfect 'just for me' supper.

Serves 1

2 parsnips, peeled and sliced thinly
1 teaspoon wholegrain mustard
2 teaspoons reduced-sugar orange marmalade
150 g (5½ oz) skinless boneless chicken breast
1 tablespoon low fat fromage frais
1 teaspoon chopped fresh chives or parsley
salt and freshly ground black pepper

10 ProPoints values per serving
10 ProPoints values per recipe

C **300 calories** per serving

Takes **25 minutes**

✱ recommended

1 Preheat the grill to medium high. Bring a pan of water to the boil and cook the parsnips for 15 minutes or until tender.

2 In a small bowl, mix the mustard and marmalade together.

3 Meanwhile, place the chicken, upper side face down, in a foil lined grill tray. Season. Grill for 8–10 minutes, then turn the chicken over and spread on the mustard and marmalade. Cook for a further 8–10 minutes or until the chicken is tender and the glaze has turned a deep golden colour.

4 Drain the cooked parsnips. Mash with the fromage frais and chopped chives or parsley. Slice the chicken and serve piled on top of the mash.

Tip There is a wonderful selection of mustards to look out for. It's a good idea to keep one or two varieties handy in the store cupboard.

Spicy Grilled Sardines

This is the sort of dish that is popular in coastal villages all around the Mediterranean. Serve with 30 g (1¼ oz) dried couscous per person, cooked according to packet instructions, and salad, for an extra 3 **ProPoints** values per serving.

Serves 4

4 garlic cloves, crushed
½ teaspoon paprika
1 teaspoon ground cumin
1 tablespoon lemon juice
2 teaspoons olive oil
12–16 (about 600 g/1 lb 5 oz) fresh sardines, cleaned
salt and freshly ground black pepper

C. **7 ProPoints** values per serving
28 ProPoints values per recipe

C **145 calories** per serving

⊘ Takes **10 minutes**

✳ not recommended

1 Preheat the grill to high.

2 Mix the garlic with the spices, lemon juice, olive oil and seasoning. Brush this mixture all over the sardines to coat thoroughly.

3 Place the sardines on a rack over the grill pan. Grill for approximately 2 minutes on each side until cooked through.

Tip One of the easiest ways to make the paste is to put the whole garlic cloves, spices, lemon juice and olive oil in a pestle and mortar and pulvarise together.

Variation This recipe can be made with 4 x 120 g (4½ oz) canned sardines in brine in exactly the same way, although the cooking time can be reduced to a minute on each side as the fish is already cooked and just needs to be warmed through. This could also be done in a frying pan. The **ProPoints** values will be 6 per serving.

Lamb Chops with Bashed Neeps

A deliciously simple recipe that can be on the table in half an hour. 'Neeps' is the Scottish word for turnips. Serve with fresh, zero **ProPoints** value steamed greens such as broccoli, beans or spinach.

Serves 4

8 x 60 g (2¼ oz) lamb chops, visible fat removed
low fat cooking spray
2 garlic cloves, crushed
150 ml (5 fl oz) orange juice
4 tablespoons redcurrant jelly
150 ml (5 fl oz) vegetable stock
1 tablespoon cornflour
salt and freshly ground black pepper

For the bashed neeps

450 g (1 lb) turnips, peeled and chopped
450 g (1 lb) carrots, peeled and chopped
150 ml (5 fl oz) very low fat fromage frais

13 ProPoints values per serving
50 ProPoints values per recipe

C **373 calories** per serving

Takes **30 minutes**

✱ not recommended

1 To make the bashed neeps, bring a large pan of water to the boil and cook the turnips and carrots for 20 minutes or so, until very tender. Drain and, when cooled a little, mash together with the fromage frais and seasoning.

2 Meanwhile, preheat the grill to medium high. Place the chops on a grill pan and season. Spray a small, non stick pan with the cooking spray and fry the garlic for a minute or so, until golden. Add the orange juice, redcurrant jelly and stock. Heat, stirring, until the jelly has dissolved. Mix the cornflour with 2 tablespoons of cold water to make a paste, then add to the other ingredients in the pan. Bring the sauce to the boil, stirring until it thickens. Season.

3 Meanwhile grill the chops for 3–4 minutes on each side until golden, seasoning when you turn them.

4 Serve the chops with the bashed neeps and sauce.

Superquick Spinach and Cheese Lasagne

Not just for vegetarians, this makes a delicious change from traditional lasagne.

Serves 2

low fat cooking spray

200 g (7 oz) frozen spinach, defrosted and drained

100 g (3½ oz) low fat soft cheese with garlic and herbs

6 sheets no pre cook lasagne (each approximately 100 g/3½ oz)

400 g can chopped tomatoes

50 g (1¾ oz) low fat Cheddar cheese, grated

salt and freshly ground black pepper

a handful of fresh basil or parsley, to garnish, optional

---

8 ProPoints values per serving
17 ProPoints values per recipe

C 686 calories per serving

Takes **5 minutes** to prepare, **20 minutes** to cook

V

✱ not recommended

1 Preheat the oven to Gas Mark 4/180°C/fan oven 160°C. Spray a small ovenproof dish with the cooking spray.

2 In a bowl, mix together the spinach and soft cheese and season with black pepper. Place two sheets of lasagne in the oven dish, then spoon over half the spinach mixture.

3 Place two more sheets of lasagne on top and spoon the remaining spinach mixture on to it. Repeat with the last two sheets, pour over the chopped tomatoes, season generously and sprinkle with the grated cheese.

4 Bake for 20 minutes or until golden and bubbling. Garnish with basil or parsley, if using.

Mussels with Tarragon

Mussels are far easier to cook than you might think and a perfect quick dish for a spontaneous dinner party.

Serves 4

low fat cooking spray
4 large shallots, chopped finely
2 garlic cloves, chopped finely
2 kg (4 lb 8 oz) fresh mussels, cleaned (see Tip)
300 ml (10 fl oz) vegetable stock
**a small bunch of fresh tarragon, tough stalks
   removed and leaves chopped**
salt and freshly ground black pepper

4 ProPoints values per serving
15 ProPoints values per recipe

185 calories per serving

Takes **20 minutes**

* not recommended

1 Spray a large, lidded pan with the cooking spray and fry the shallots and garlic until softened, adding a little water, if necessary, to stop them sticking.

2 Add the mussels and stock and cover the pan. Cook over a high heat for 3–4 minutes, or until all the mussels have opened, shaking the pan every now and then. Discard any mussels that have remained shut during cooking.

3 Lift the mussels out of the cooking liquid with a slotted spoon and divide them between four serving bowls.

4 Strain the cooking liquid into a small pan and add the tarragon. Boil for a few minutes until reduced a little, check the seasoning and then pour over the mussels to serve.

Tip To prepare mussels, scrub off any dirt and remove any barnacles. Remove the beard, if any, that sticks out between the shells. Discard any mussels that are already open or have a cracked shell.

Chick Pea and Vegetable Curry

A great panful of curry for feeding a crowd; the chick peas really take on the spicy flavours of the sauce. Serve with 60 g (2 oz) dried brown rice per person, cooked according to packet instructions, for an extra 6 *ProPoints* values per serving. Any leftovers taste even better the next day.

Serves 6

400 g (14 oz) potatoes, peeled and diced
2 large carrots, peeled and diced
250 g (9 oz) cauliflower, broken into florets
150 g (5½ oz) green beans, halved
low fat cooking spray
1 onion, chopped
2 tablespoons curry paste
400 g can chopped tomatoes
150 g (5½ oz) low fat natural yogurt
410 g can chick peas, rinsed and drained
**2 tablespoons chopped fresh coriander,
   to garnish**

1 Bring a large pan of water to the boil and cook the potatoes and carrots for 5 minutes. Add the cauliflower and green beans and cook for 5 minutes more then drain the vegetables.

2 Meanwhile, heat a large, non stick pan, spray with the cooking spray and brown the onion, adding a splash of water, if needed, to stop it from sticking. Stir in the curry paste and cook for 1 minute, then add the tomatoes and yogurt.

3 Mix the vegetables and chick peas into the curry sauce and cook for 10 minutes. Serve topped with the chopped coriander.

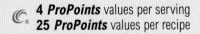

4 *ProPoints* values per serving
25 *ProPoints* values per recipe

C **179 calories** per serving

⏱ Takes **30 minutes**

V

✳ not recommended

Seville Orange-glazed Duck with Marsala and Cranberry Sauce

Serves 4

1 tablespoon olive oil

2 x 150 g (5½ oz) skinless boneless duck breasts

4 tablespoons Marsala wine

150 ml (5 fl oz) hot chicken stock

zest of an orange, pared and cut into fine shreds

75 g (2¾ oz) cranberries, fresh or thawed if frozen

1 tablespoon Seville orange marmalade

salt and freshly ground black pepper

1 Heat the oil in a large, non stick frying pan. Add the duck breasts and sear over a medium high heat for 2 minutes on each side, until browned.

2 Add the Marsala, allowing it to bubble up in the pan. Pour in the stock, bring to the boil, then turn down the heat slightly. Add the orange shreds and continue to cook until the liquid has reduced by half, about 8–10 minutes.

3 Add the cranberries and marmalade to the frying pan, stirring gently until the marmalade has melted. Simmer for 2–3 more minutes to cook the cranberries. Season to taste, then serve.

10 *ProPoints* values per serving
21 *ProPoints* values per recipe

C **325 calories** per serving

Takes **5 minutes** to prepare, **20 minutes** to cook

✱ not recommended

Variation Use sherry instead of the Marsala, if you prefer. The *ProPoints* values will remain the same.

Vietnamese Beef and Noodle Stir Fry

If you like it extra hot, leave the seeds in the chilli.

Serves 4

250 g (9 oz) dried rice noodles
low fat cooking spray
400 g (14 oz) lean beef medallion steak, sliced thinly
1 red onion, sliced thinly
2 garlic cloves, sliced
1 red chilli, de-seeded and sliced
250 g (9 oz) beansprouts, rinsed and drained
juice of ½ a lime
3 tablespoons soy sauce
½ x 25 g packet fresh coriander, sprigs left whole

---

11 *ProPoints* values per serving
44 *ProPoints* values per recipe

432 calories per serving

Takes **15 minutes**

not recommended

1 Bring a pan of water to the boil and add the noodles. Return to the boil then remove immediately from the heat. Leave to stand for 3 minutes while the noodles soften, then drain and rinse in cold water. Drain again.

2 Meanwhile, heat a wok or large, non stick frying pan and spray with the cooking spray. Stir fry the sliced steak over a high heat for 3 minutes, then transfer to a plate.

3 Add the onion, garlic and chilli to the pan and stir fry for 2 minutes. Mix in the beansprouts, followed by the noodles, beef, lime juice and soy sauce. Stir fry for 2 minutes until piping hot and well mixed. Mix in the sprigs of coriander just before serving.

Nasi Goreng

Nasi goreng means 'fried rice' in Indonesia, where it is enjoyed as a quick family meal.

Serves 4

240 g (8½ oz) dried rice
4 teaspoons Indonesian or Thai red curry paste
250 g (9 oz) pork fillet, cut into thin strips
200 g (7 oz) frozen cooked, peeled prawns, thawed
1 tablespoon soy sauce
200 g (7 oz) frozen petit pois, defrosted
2 eggs, beaten
a small bunch of fresh coriander, chopped, to garnish

---

12 *ProPoints* values per serving
47 *ProPoints* values per recipe

C **430 calories** per serving

Takes **15 minutes**

✻ not recommended

1 Bring a pan of water to the boil and cook the rice according to the packet instructions. Drain and rinse thoroughly. Set aside.

2 Meanwhile, heat the curry paste in a wok or large, non stick frying pan then add the pork and stir fry for 4–5 minutes, until cooked through.

3 Add all the other ingredients, except the eggs and coriander but including the rice, and stir fry for 5 minutes then push everything to one side of the wok or pan and pour in the eggs. Stir until lightly set like scrambled egg, then stir in the other ingredients.

4 Scatter with the coriander and serve.

Turkey Steaks with Caramelised Apples

A really flavoursome dish of succulent turkey and golden apple wedges in a delicious sauce. Serve with green cabbage, for no additional *ProPoints* values per serving.

Serves 2

15 g (½ oz) low fat spread
1 tablespoon caster sugar
2 apples, cored and each cut into 6–8 wedges
low fat cooking spray
2 x 125 g (4½ oz) turkey breast steaks
1 small onion, chopped finely
150 ml (5 fl oz) apple juice
1 tablespoon cider vinegar
50 g (1¾ oz) half fat crème fraîche
salt and freshly ground black pepper

3 *ProPoints* values per serving
14 *ProPoints* values per recipe

461 calories per serving

Takes **25 minutes**

✱ not recommended

1 Melt the low fat spread and sugar in a large, non stick frying pan. Add the apple wedges and fry for about 3 minutes on each side over a high heat until golden and lightly caramelised. Remove to a plate.

2 Spray the frying pan with the cooking spray and season the turkey steaks. Fry for 3 minutes, then turn, scattering the onion around the turkey.

3 Fry for a further 3 minutes, stirring the onion once or twice, then pour in the apple juice and cider vinegar.

4 Bubble for 2 minutes, then stir in the crème fraîche and apples to warm through for about 30 seconds before serving.

Oven-roasted Tomatoes with Goat's Cheese

This delicious supper dish is best served with a 50 g (1¾ oz) brown crusty roll and a fresh green salad of rocket or another peppery leaf like watercress, for an additional 4 **ProPoints** values.

Serves 1

100 g (3½ oz) vine-ripened small tomatoes, still on the vine
50 g (1¾ oz) small 'crotin' goat's cheese
2 teaspoons balsamic vinegar
salt and freshly ground black pepper

4 **ProPoints** values per serving
4 **ProPoints** values per recipe

C 170 **calories** per serving

Takes **10 minutes**

V

✱ not recommended

1 Preheat the oven to Gas Mark 7/220°C/fan oven 200°C and place the tomatoes and goat's cheese on a non stick baking tray. Roast for 5–10 minutes, until the cheese is soft and golden and the tomatoes are beginning to soften.

2 Place the cheese and tomatoes on a serving plate and drizzle with the balsamic vinegar. Season and serve.

Tip When you are cooking for one, opt for something quick and easy such as this recipe. It feels special but doesn't take too long – leaving you more time to pamper yourself.

Chinese Ginger Noodles

Serve this dish as soon as you make it otherwise the noodles soak up too much of the sauce and become stodgy.

Serves 4

225 g (8 oz) dried thin egg noodles

2 teaspoons vegetable oil

225 g (8 oz) carrots, peeled and cut into matchsticks

5 cm (2 inch) fresh root ginger, peeled and grated

2 garlic cloves, chopped

225 g (8 oz) firm tofu, diced

6 spring onions, sliced into long, thin strips

150 g (5½ oz) fresh beansprouts

100 ml (3½ fl oz) vegetable stock

1 teaspoon cornflour

2 tablespoons soy sauce

1 tablespoon tomato purée

25 g (1 oz) cashew nuts, chopped roughly, to garnish

© **10 ProPoints** values per serving
   39 ProPoints values per recipe

C **360 calories** per serving

⊘ Takes **25 minutes**

V

✳ recommended

1 Place the noodles in a bowl and cover with boiling water. Leave to stand for 10 minutes, stirring from time to time to separate them. Drain thoroughly.

2 Heat the oil in a large, non stick frying pan or wok and add the carrots, ginger and garlic. Stir fry for 2–3 minutes and then mix in the tofu, spring onions and beansprouts. Stir fry for a further 2 minutes.

3 Add the noodles to the pan with the stock. Mix well and heat through for 2 minutes.

4 Mix together the cornflour, soy sauce and tomato purée and add this to the pan. Cook, stirring, until the sauce thickens.

5 Pile into a warmed serving bowl and scatter with the chopped cashew nuts. Serve hot.

Tip Keep a piece of root ginger in the freezer and you'll always have some to hand; it also grates more easily when frozen.

French Ham and Bean Casserole (Cassoulet)

Cassoulet is a bean and tomato-based casserole from the Languedoc region in France. This is a very quick cheat's version.

Serves 4

low fat cooking spray
2 onions, chopped
3 garlic cloves, crushed
400 g can chopped tomatoes
2 tablespoons tomato purée
2 sprigs thyme, woody stems removed, chopped
2 sprigs marjoram, chopped
1 celery stick, sliced finely
1 bay leaf
200 g (7 oz) thick sliced lean ham, cubed
2 x 300 g cans haricot beans, rinsed and drained
a small bunch of fresh parsley, chopped
salt and freshly ground black pepper

3 *ProPoints* values per serving
13 *ProPoints* values per recipe

225 calories per serving

Takes **10 minutes** to prepare,
15 minutes to cook

not recommended

1 Heat a large, non stick frying pan and spray with the cooking spray. Fry the onions and garlic for 5 minutes until softened, adding a few tablespoons of water to prevent them from sticking, if necessary.

2 Add the tomatoes and tomato purée, thyme, marjoram, celery and bay leaf and bring to the boil. Season and simmer for 10 minutes until thick.

3 Add the ham and beans and simmer for a further 5 minutes. Remove the bay leaf, stir in the parsley and serve.

Pork with Tomatoes and Red Wine

Serve with 60 g (2 oz) dried rice per person, cooked according to packet instructions, and fresh steamed vegetables, for an extra 6 *ProPoints* values per serving.

Serves 4

350 g (12 oz) pork tenderloin, cut into strips
1 large onion, chopped
400 g can chopped tomatoes with herbs
150 ml (5 fl oz) red wine
1 tablespoon tomato purée
150 ml (5 fl oz) hot vegetable or chicken stock
1 teaspoon dried herbes de Provence or Italian mixed herbs
225 g (8 oz) chestnut or open cap mushrooms, halved
2 courgettes, sliced thickly
1 teaspoon dried sage
2 teaspoons cornflour
salt and freshly ground black pepper

---

4 *ProPoints* values per serving
16 *ProPoints* values per recipe

C **220 calories** per serving

Takes **10 minutes** to prepare,
20 minutes to cook

✱ not recommended

1 Heat a large, lidded, non stick frying pan and dry fry the pork and onion for 5 minutes then stir in the tomatoes, red wine, tomato purée, stock, herbs, mushrooms, courgettes and sage. Bring to the boil, then cover and simmer for 15 minutes.

2 Blend the cornflour to a paste with 2 tablespoons of cold water and stir into the pork mixture. Simmer, uncovered, for 1–2 minutes to thicken the sauce. Season to taste. Serve.

Tip Bulk this out for the family with additional chopped vegetables such as carrots, celery and leeks for a hearty and filling casserole, for no additional *ProPoints* values.

Mexican Beef and Bean Mince

This recipe uses loads of spices to boost the flavour while minimising preparation and cooking times. It is delicious served with 60 g (2 oz) dried brown rice per person, cooked according to packet instructions, for 6 extra *ProPoints* values per serving, or rolled up in lettuce leaves with chopped tomato and cucumber, for no additional *ProPoints* values per serving.

Serves 4

low fat cooking spray
1 garlic clove, crushed
1 onion, chopped finely
1 carrot, peeled and chopped finely
1 red, green or yellow pepper, de-seeded and chopped finely
500 g (1 lb 2 oz) extra lean beef mince
2 x 400 g cans tomatoes, chopped
2 teaspoons chilli powder
¼ teaspoon dried oregano
1 teaspoon artificial sweetener
410 g can pinto beans, rinsed and drained
salt and freshly ground black pepper

8 *ProPoints* values per serving
31 *ProPoints* values per recipe

C **299 calories** per serving

Takes **15 minutes** to prepare,
15 minutes to cook

✳ recommended (up to 3 months)

1 Spray a large, non stick frying pan with the cooking spray and place over a medium high heat. Add the garlic, onion, carrot and pepper and cook, stirring, for 5 minutes or until the vegetables are tender.

2 Increase the heat to high and add the mince. Cook, stirring, for 5 minutes, breaking up any clumps with the back of a wooden spoon. Season to taste.

3 Add the tomatoes, chilli powder, oregano, sweetener and beans. Check the seasoning. Reduce the heat to medium low and simmer for 10 minutes or until the sauce thickens.

Tips You can always add more or less chilli to create the desired effect.

Any leftovers can be stored in an airtight container in the fridge for 2–3 days and reheated in a microwave or oven.

Home Baked Breaded Fish

Serve with an 80 g (3 oz) portion of cooked peas per person, for an extra 2 *ProPoints* value per serving.

Serves 4

low fat cooking spray
1 egg, beaten
40 g (1½ oz) fresh breadcrumbs
1 tablespoon chopped fresh parsley
finely grated zest of a lemon, plus wedges to
   serve
4 x 125 g (4½ oz) skinless coley fillets
450 g (1 lb) new potatoes, halved if large
350 g (12 oz) broccoli, cut into florets
salt and freshly ground black pepper

For the tartare sauce
150 g pot 0% fat Greek yogurt
1 tablespoon reduced fat mayonnaise
40 g (1½ oz) gherkins, diced

7 *ProPoints* values per serving
26 *ProPoints* values per recipe

C **301 calories** per serving

Takes **10 minutes** to prepare,
15 minutes to cook

✱ recommended (fish only)

1 Preheat the oven to Gas Mark 7/220°C/fan oven 200°C. Spray a baking tray with the cooking spray.

2 Place the egg in a shallow bowl. In a seperate shallow bowl or plate, mix together the breadcrumbs with the parsley and lemon zest and a little seasoning. Dip the fish fillets into the egg first and then into the breadcrumbs, coating both sides. Place on the baking tray and spray with the cooking spray. Cook for 10–15 minutes, turning once until golden on both sides.

3 Meanwhile, bring a pan of water to the boil, add the potatoes and cook for 10–12 minutes until tender. Add the broccoli for the final 3 minutes of cooking time. Drain.

4 To make the tartare sauce, mix together all the ingredients with a little black pepper. Serve a fillet of fish each with the vegetables and tartare sauce divided evenly between the four plates, and with a lemon wedge to squeeze over.

Tip Visit your local fishmonger or the supermarket counter so you can choose your own fish and specify what you want. They should bone and skin it for you too. And look out for frozen fillets in the freezer section as these are good value.

Lamb Steak Provençale

The wonderful fresh tomato and courgette sauce in this recipe complements lamb perfectly, drawing out its delicate flavours. This is delicious served with 100 g (3½ oz) thick cut, oven baked chips, for an extra 5 *ProPoints* values.

Serves 1

2 fresh tomatoes
a kettleful of boiling water
1 large garlic clove, crushed
2 spring onions, chopped
1 courgette, chopped
3 tablespoons dry white wine
1 sprig of fresh basil, chopped or ½ teaspoon
  dried basil
125 g (4½ oz) lean lamb leg steak
salt and freshly ground black pepper

7 *ProPoints* values per serving
7 *ProPoints* values per recipe

C **229 calories** per serving

Takes **10 minutes** to prepare,
20 minutes to cook

* not recommended

1 With a sharp knife, score small crosses in the base of the tomatoes then place them in a bowl of just boiled water. Remove them after 30 seconds and slip off the skins. Quarter the tomatoes, remove the seeds and chop the flesh.

2 Place the tomatoes in a medium size, lidded saucepan with the garlic, spring onions, courgette, wine and seasoning. If you are using dried basil, add it at this stage. Cook the mixture until it sizzles. Reduce the heat, cover and simmer gently for 10 minutes until the vegetables have softened. If you are using fresh basil, mix it in at this stage.

3 Meanwhile, preheat the grill. Season the lamb steak and grill for about 5 minutes on each side. Alternatively, you can cook it on a non stick griddle pan. If you like the lamb slightly pink, cook it until it feels lightly springy, or, if you like it well done, cook it until the meat is firm.

4 Spoon the sauce over the lamb to serve.

Tip Use this sauce for pasta. Make a double quantity and freeze in two single portions.

Tagliatelle with Lentil and Mushroom Sauce

Lentils are great for a quick and nourishing meat-free meal, and they taste particularly good in this pasta sauce. Serve it with freshly cooked zero **ProPoints** value cabbage or green beans.

Serves 4

1 large onion, chopped
2 teaspoons garlic purée
1 carrot, peeled and grated coarsely
250 g (9 oz) mushrooms, chopped finely
2 teaspoons olive oil
½ teaspoon dried oregano or marjoram
230 g can chopped tomatoes
400 g can red lentils, rinsed and drained
200 g (7 oz) dried tagliatelle
salt and freshly ground black pepper

To serve
4 tablespoons Quark
2 teaspoons freshly grated Parmesan cheese

---

 9 ProPoints values per serving
35 ProPoints values per recipe

C **340 calories** per serving

⊙ Takes **10 minutes** to prepare,
20 minutes to cook

V

✳ recommended for the sauce

1 Mix the onion, garlic purée, carrot, mushrooms and olive oil in a large, lidded pan then add 4 tablespoons of water. Heat this mixture until it sizzles. Cover the pan and simmer for 10 minutes until the vegetables have softened, stirring once or twice.

2 Season and add the herbs, tomatoes and lentils. Cook, uncovered, until all the liquid has evaporated and the mixture has thickened – this will take about 10 minutes. Check the seasoning.

3 Meanwhile, bring a pan of water to the boil and cook the tagliatelle according to the packet instructions. Drain and mix it with the sauce. Serve in four warmed bowls and top each serving of pasta with 1 tablespoon of Quark and ½ teaspoon of Parmesan cheese.

Stuffed Chicken Breasts

A simple, classic recipe that is wonderful served with Mediterranean style roasted vegetables, or just some grilled tomatoes, for no extra *ProPoints* values per serving.

Serves 4

50 g (1¾ oz) smoked ham, diced
2 teaspoons snipped chives
100 g (½ oz) low fat soft cheese
4 x 165 g (5¾ oz) skinless boneless chicken
 breasts
low fat cooking spray
salt and freshly ground black pepper

5 ProPoints values per serving
21 ProPoints values per recipe

C **170 calories** per serving

Takes **10 minutes** to prepare,
15 minutes to cook

✳ not recommended

1 Preheat the oven to Gas Mark 6/200°C/ fan oven 180°C.

2 Mix the ham, chives and seasoning into the low fat soft cheese.

3 Using a small sharp knife, make a pocket along the length of each chicken breast, taking care not to cut right through. Fill with the stuffing then place the chicken breasts in a small roasting tin and spray with a little cooking spray.

4 Roast for 15 minutes or until the chicken is cooked through; the juices should run clear when the thickest part of the chicken is pierced.

Ginger and Mustard Pork

Quick and easy, this is a perfect dish for a midweek meal.

Serves 2

250 g (9 oz) pork escalopes, each cut into
  6–8 pieces
low fat cooking spray
1 red onion, sliced into rings
3 slices of fresh root ginger, peeled and each
  about the size of a pound coin
1 garlic clove, crushed
150 ml (5 fl oz) chicken stock
1 teaspoon Tabasco
2 teaspoons wholegrain mustard
1 tablespoon maple syrup
salt and freshly ground black pepper

6 **ProPoints** values per serving
13 **ProPoints** values per recipe

C 213 calories per serving

Takes **10 minutes** to prepare,
15 minutes to cook

✱ not recommended

1 Heat a large, non stick frying pan to a high temperature and quickly brown the pork pieces on both sides. (You won't need any cooking spray at this stage.) Remove the pork and keep warm on a covered plate.

2 Reduce the heat of the pan, spray it with the cooking spray and add the onion, ginger and garlic. Cook for 3–5 minutes until soft and starting to brown.

3 Add the stock, Tabasco and mustard, bring to a gentle simmer and then return the pork to the pan. Cook for 5–10 minutes until the pork is cooked through.

4 Remove the slices of ginger and stir in the maple syrup. Season to taste and serve on warmed plates.

Sweet Tooth

Try these fast and fabulous desserts and bakes when you're in the mood for something sweet. From Spicy Nectarines to Apple Bread Pudding, and from Cherry Brûlée to Poached Meringues with Raspberry Coulis, there is something here to suit everyone.

Sweet and sensational — for when you fancy a treat

Paradise Pudding

This simple pudding is bound to become an all-time favourite and friends will ask you for the recipe whenever you make it.

Serves 4

4 digestive biscuits, crushed
4 tablespoons medium or sweet sherry
350 g (12 oz) seedless red and green grapes, halved
200 g (7 oz) low fat soft cheese
150 g (5½ oz) low fat natural yogurt
½ teaspoon vanilla extract
4 heaped teaspoons demerara sugar

 5 *ProPoints* values per serving
21 *ProPoints* values per recipe

C **300 calories** per serving

⏲ Takes **20 minutes** + **10 minutes** chilling

V

✳ not recommended

1 Sprinkle half the biscuit crumbs into four ramekin dishes or ovenproof cups and sprinkle with half the sherry.

2 Mix the red and green grapes together and spoon half of them into the dishes or cups.

3 Beat the cheese with a wooden spoon to soften it, then mix in the yogurt and vanilla extract. Spoon half of it over the desserts. Repeat all the layers once more. Chill the desserts for 10 minutes.

4 Preheat a hot grill. Sprinkle 1 heaped teaspoon of sugar over each dessert and mist lightly with water (this helps the sugar to dissolve quickly under the grill). Place the ramekins under the grill until the sugar melts and bubbles, then allow to cool. Chill until ready to serve.

Variation Instead of using demerara sugar, substitute unrefined light or dark muscovado sugar. There's no need to grill it, just leave it for about 10 minutes and it will melt. The ***ProPoints*** values will remain the same.

Light Date and Banana Pudding

This delicious dessert is great for when you're on your own and crave something sweet.

Serves 1

1 banana
a few drops of lemon juice
1 egg, separated
1 tablespoon skimmed milk
15 g (½ oz) dates, chopped
a pinch of ground nutmeg
2 teaspoons caster sugar

4 ProPoints values per serving
4 ProPoints values per recipe

C **295 calories** per serving

Takes **10 minutes** to prepare,
20 minutes to bake

V

✳ not recommended

1 Preheat the oven to Gas Mark 5/190°C/fan oven 170°C.

2 In a medium size bowl, mash the banana with the lemon juice then mix in the egg yolk, milk, dates and nutmeg. Transfer the mixture to a small, ovenproof dish and bake for 10–15 minutes until lightly set.

3 In a clean, grease-free bowl, beat the egg white until stiff then whisk in the sugar to form a stiff, glossy meringue mixture. Pile this on top of the banana base then cook for another 5 minutes until golden. Serve at once.

Orange Jaffa Surprise

If you are a fan of Jaffa cakes, you will find this idea a tasty way to make a couple go further. Leave this dessert to chill while the flavours are absorbed by the sponge base.

Serves 2

4 Jaffa cakes, diced
1 orange
150 g (5½ oz) low fat ready-to-eat custard

4 ProPoints values per serving
8 ProPoints values per recipe

180 calories per serving

Takes **5 minutes** + **10 minutes** chilling

V

* not recommended

1 Divide the Jaffa cakes between two glass sundae dishes.

2 Peel and segment the orange over a bowl so that you can catch the juice. Chop the segments into pieces and scatter over the Jaffa cakes. Then pour on the reserved orange juice.

3 Spoon the custard evenly over the oranges. Chill for 10 minutes.

Cinnamon Tortilla Chips with Berry Salsa

This unusual sweet version of tortilla chips and salsa is a great dessert to share.

Serves 4

25 g (1 oz) caster sugar
1 teaspoon ground cinnamon
3 soft flour tortillas
low fat cooking spray
100 g (3½ oz) raspberries
200 g (7 oz) strawberries, trimmed and diced
75 g (2¾ oz) blueberries
150 g (5½ oz) 0% fat Greek yogurt

4 ProPoints values per serving
15 ProPoints values per recipe

C **168 calories** per serving

Takes **15 minutes**

V

✻ not recommended

1 Preheat the oven to Gas Mark 4/180°C/fan oven 160°C.

2 In a bowl, mix together the sugar and cinnamon. Measure out 2 teaspoons for the salsa and transfer to another bowl.

3 Spray both sides of each tortilla with the cooking spray and sprinkle with the cinnamon sugar. Using kitchen scissors, cut each tortilla into four strips then snip the strips into small triangles. Spread out on a large baking tray and bake for 6–7 minutes until crisp.

4 To make the berry salsa, put the raspberries into a bowl with the reserved cinnamon sugar and lightly crush using a fork. Stir in the strawberries and the whole blueberries.

5 Serve the berry salsa with the cinnamon tortilla chips for dipping and the yogurt on the side.

Banana, Kiwi and Mango Cocktail

This colourful fruit cocktail has a zingy citrus kick to it.

Serves 4

1 large mango, peeled, stoned and sliced
2 kiwi fruit, peeled and sliced
2 bananas, peeled and sliced
8 tablespoons lime and lemongrass cordial
8 tablespoons low fat natural yogurt

To decorate
lime zest
mint leaves

1 Mix together all the fruits and divide them between four serving bowls or glasses.

2 Dilute the cordial with 200 ml (7 fl oz) of cold water. Pour over the fruit and leave for at least 15 minutes before serving.

3 Serve with 2 tablespoons of yogurt per portion. Decorate with lime zest and mint leaves.

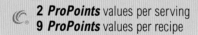

2 ProPoints values per serving
9 ProPoints values per recipe

C 150 calories per serving

Takes **15 minutes**
+ **15 minutes** resting

V

✱ not recommended

Tip If you can't find lime and lemongrass cordial, substitute elderflower cordial instead, adding a squeeze of lime or lemon juice. The **ProPoints** values will remain the same.

Variations If you're making this fruit salad for a Christmas or New Year celebration, why not add a thinly sliced star fruit to make it look really festive? The **ProPoints** values will remain the same.

Poached Meringues with Raspberry Coulis

You could use fresh raspberries for this light dessert if they are in season.

Serves 4

250 g (9 oz) frozen raspberries, defrosted
1½ teaspoons orange juice

3 tablespoons artificial sweetener
2 egg whites
grated zest of an orange

1 Using a food processor or a hand held blender, whizz the raspberries to a purée with the orange juice. Press through a sieve to remove the seeds then stir in 1 tablespoon of the sweetener. Divide between four shallow bowls.

2 Bring a frying pan of water to the boil. In a clean, grease-free bowl, whisk the egg whites until stiff then beat in the remaining sweetener and 1 teaspoon of the orange zest.

3 Dip an ice cream scoop into a jug of cold water, then take a scoop of meringue and push it into the pan of water. Repeat to make four meringues from half the mixture. Poach for 1 minute on each side.

4 With a draining spoon, lift the meringues out of the water and place one in each bowl. Repeat with the remaining mixture to make four more meringues. Serve garnished with the rest of the orange zest.

0 ProPoints values per serving
0 ProPoints values per recipe

41 calories per serving

Takes **15 minutes**

V

✳ not recommended

Apple Bread Pudding

This is best made with slightly stale bread, so it's ideal for using up the end of a loaf in the bread bin. Instead of buying apple sauce, you can make it by chopping an apple, cooking it in a little water and then mashing it.

Serves 4

low fat cooking spray
200 g (7 oz) low fat vanilla flavour yogurt
1 egg, beaten
½ teaspoon ground mixed spice
100 g (3½ oz) apple sauce
25 g (1 oz) soft light brown sugar
100 g (3½ oz) crustless white or wholemeal
  bread, diced
1 apple, cored and diced

4 ProPoints values per serving
17 ProPoints values per recipe

C **181 calories** per serving

Takes **5 minutes** to prepare,
25 minutes to bake

V

❋ not recommended

1 Preheat the oven to Gas Mark 4/180°C/fan oven 160°C. Spray a baking dish with the cooking spray.

2 Reserve half the yogurt to serve. In a bowl, mix the remaining yogurt together with the beaten egg, mixed spice, apple sauce and sugar.

3 Stir the bread into the mixture, mixing well to coat, then stir in the apple. Spoon into the baking dish and bake in the oven for 25 minutes until firm, with a golden brown crispy top.

4 Serve hot with the reserved vanilla yogurt drizzled over.

Honey and Brandy Roasted Figs

Fig desserts like this one are elegant and need almost no dressing up – a great choice for supper parties.

Serves 6

12 fresh figs
50 ml (2 fl oz) brandy
6 teaspoons reduced sugar apricot jam, sieved
4 tablespoons runny honey
6 tablespoons 0% fat Greek yogurt, to serve

3 *ProPoints* values per serving
16 *ProPoints* values per recipe

106 calories per serving

Takes **7 minutes** to prepare,
10 minutes to cook

V

✳ not recommended

1 Preheat the oven to Gas Mark 8/230°C/fan oven 210°C.

2 Place the figs in a shallow, ovenproof dish. In a small bowl, stir together the brandy, jam and honey. Drizzle the figs with half of the brandy mixture.

3 Roast the figs for 5 minutes. Drizzle with the remaining brandy mixture and roast for a further 5 minutes. Allow to cool for about 5 minutes.

4 Place 2 figs in each of six small serving dishes. Drizzle with a spoonful of brandy mixture from the baking dish and add a dollop of yogurt to serve.

Raspberry Atholl Brose

Atholl Brose is a traditional Scottish oatmeal dessert made with a tot of Scotch whisky. This light version is perfect for Burns Night.

Serves 4

50 g (1¾ oz) porridge oats
25 g (1 oz) muscovado or demerara sugar
1 heaped teaspoon honey
45 ml (1¾ fl oz) whisky
200 g (7 oz) 0% fat Greek yogurt
200 g (7 oz) frozen raspberries, thawed

4 ProPoints values per serving
15 ProPoints values per recipe

137 calories per serving

Takes **15 minutes** to prepare + chilling
5 minutes to cook

V

✳ not recommended

1 Preheat the grill to medium. Sprinkle the porridge oats on to a baking sheet and grill until lightly browned, turning occasionally using a spatula. Let them cool.

2 Mix the porridge oats with the sugar. Stir the honey and whisky together. Fold the oats and honey mixtures through the yogurt.

3 Lightly crush the raspberries with a fork. Tip them into the oat mixture and partially fold through. Spoon into serving glasses, then cover and chill until ready to serve.

Cherry Brûlée

Quark is a very low fat soft cheese that is ideal for making desserts.

Serves 2

150 g (5½ oz) cherries, stoned
125 g (4½ oz) Quark
100 g (3½ oz) very low fat plain fromage frais
½ teaspoon vanilla extract
50 g (1¾ oz) demerara sugar

5 *ProPoints* values per serving
9 *ProPoints* values per recipe

C **175 calories** per serving

Takes **10 minutes**

V

✳ not recommended

1 Preheat the grill to its highest setting.

2 Place the cherries in the base of two ramekins. Whisk the Quark and fromage frais together with the vanilla extract until smooth. Spoon on top of the fruit and level the surface.

3 Sprinkle the sugar evenly over the top and mist lightly with water (this helps the sugar to dissolve quickly under the grill). Pop under the hot grill and cook for 2–3 minutes until the sugar has melted and begun to caramelise.

4 Allow the brûlées to cool, and the caramel to harden, for a couple of minutes before serving.

Tip You can use an olive stoner to stone cherries if you have one but, if not, place the cherries on a chopping board and lightly crush with a rolling pin or filled can to release the stones.

Creamy Blackcurrant Crunch

A crunchy sweet texture tops a layer of creamy fromage frais, which in turn hides a delicious layer of flavour packed blackcurrants.

Serves 4

300 g (10½ oz) canned blackcurrants in natural juice, drained
3 tablespoons reduced sugar blackcurrant jam
300 g (10½ oz) low fat plain fromage frais
50 g (1¾ oz) crunchy oat cereal
2 teaspoons clear honey

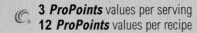 **3 *ProPoints*** values per serving
12 *ProPoints* values per recipe

C **140 calories** per serving

Takes **20 minutes**

V

* not recommended

1 Place the blackcurrants and jam in a small saucepan over a low heat for 2–3 minutes, until the jam melts and coats the blackcurrants.

2 Divide the mixture between four individual glasses and top each one with a layer of fromage frais.

3 Crumble the crunchy oat cereal over the top of each one and then finally drizzle the surface with a little honey.

Variation You can vary the fruit in this dish – try fresh raspberries mixed with reduced sugar raspberry jam or canned apricots mixed with reduced sugar apricot jam. The *ProPoints* values remain the same.

Thai Rice Pudding

Thai rice makes a deliciously fragrant, easy to cook rice pudding in under 30 minutes. The mango complements the flavour of this dish perfectly.

Serves 4

2 tablespoons desiccated coconut
750 ml (26 fl oz) skimmed milk
100 g (3½ oz) dried jasmine rice
artificial sweetener, to taste
1 fresh lemongrass stem (optional)
1 ripe mango, peeled, stoned and sliced thinly, to serve

5 *ProPoints* values per serving
20 *ProPoints* values per recipe

C **225 calories** per serving

Takes **15 minutes** to prepare,
15 minutes to cook

V

✻ not recommended

1 In a medium saucepan, heat the coconut and milk until boiling. Remove the pan from the heat and set aside to cool for 10 minutes.

2 Strain the milk mixture and then discard the coconut.

3 Meanwhile, place the rice in enough boiling water just to cover it and blanch it for 2 minutes. Drain, return the rice to the pan and add the coconut flavoured milk and sweetener.

4 With a sharp knife, slash the lemongrass stem, if using, and add it to the rice. Bring the milk to the boil then reduce the heat and simmer for about 15 minutes, stirring occasionally.

5 When the rice has swollen and softened and the mixture has thickened, remove the lemongrass and allow the rice to cool.

6 Serve the rice pudding in small dishes topped with mango slices.

Tip Instead of using high fat coconut cream in recipes, make your own lower fat coconut milk by heating desiccated coconut in skimmed milk.

Variations This is equally good with fragrant basmati rice instead of jasmine rice, however, don't use the easy cook variety – it won't give you the same soft creaminess. The *ProPoints* values will remain the same.

Spicy Nectarines

Poaching fruit is often a great way to use any excess. It will keep in the fridge or you could freeze it.

Serves 4

6 nectarines or peaches, halved and stoned
1 star anise
2 tablespoons artificial sweetener, plus
  2 teaspoons
4 tablespoons low fat plain fromage frais
1 teaspoon mixed spice

---

1 *ProPoints* value per serving
2 *ProPoints* values per recipe

C **86 calories** per serving

Takes **15 minutes**

V

* recommended (fruit only)

1 Place the nectarines or peaches in a lidded saucepan with the star anise, 2 tablespoons of sweetener and 150 ml (5 fl oz) of water. Bring to the boil, cover and simmer for 10 minutes or until softened. Remove from the heat and cool slightly.

2 Mix the 2 teaspoons of sweetener into the fromage frais with the mixed spice. Serve the warm fruit and its juices with a dollop of spiced fromage frais.

Tip Cool, cover and refrigerate the fruit for up to 3 days.

Caramel Oranges with Ginger Crunch

This simple recipe has a great flavour combination.

Serves 2

25 g (1 oz) caster sugar
3 oranges
25 g (1 oz) reduced fat ginger biscuits, crushed

3 ProPoints values per serving
6 ProPoints values per recipe

238 calories per serving

Takes **15 minutes** to prepare,
10 minutes to cook

V

✳ not recommended

1 Preheat the oven to Gas Mark 4/180°C/fan oven 160°C.

2 Place the sugar in a small, heavy based pan with 2 tablespoons of water. Using a peeler, take a piece of zest (remove any white) from one of the oranges and place in the pan. Heat gently until the sugar has dissolved then increase the heat and let the syrup boil until brown. Remove from the heat and take out the piece of zest.

3 Squeeze the juice from one of the oranges (you should get about 30 ml/1¼ fl oz) and add it to the caramel, stirring to combine. Peel the remaining oranges and slice thinly. Lay down the orange in layers in an ovenproof dish. Pour over the syrup and scatter the biscuit crumbs on top. Bake for 10 minutes until bubbling and the top is darkening. Cool slightly before serving.

Tip Serve with a 60 g (2 oz) scoop of low fat ice cream per person, for an extra 2 **ProPoints** values per serving.

Crushed Lemon Meringue Layer

A crunchy zesty light dessert that is quick and easy and tastes divine.

Serves 4

300 g (10½ oz) low fat soft cheese
150 g (5½ oz) 0% fat Greek yogurt
finely grated zest and juice of a lemon
2 tablespoons artificial sweetener, or to taste
2 meringue nests, roughly crushed

To decorate
lemon slices
a few mint leaves

3 ProPoints values per serving
13 ProPoints values per recipe

143 calories per serving

Takes **15 minutes**

V

✱ not recommended

1 Beat the soft cheese and yogurt together until smooth. Add the lemon zest and juice, stirring to mix. Stir in the sweetener, adding more to suit your taste, if necessary.

2 Layer the crushed meringues and the lemon mixture in small glasses. Chill until ready to serve, then decorate with the lemon slices and mint leaves.

Baked Doughnuts

Specially shaped, moulded trays for baking doughnuts are available from good cook shops. Be careful not to overfill them otherwise the cooked doughnuts will not have any holes.

Makes 16

75 g (2¾ oz) plain flour
1 teaspoon baking powder
1 egg, beaten
1 teaspoon corn oil
½ teaspoon vanilla extract
75 g (2¾ oz) caster sugar, plus 2 teaspoons for dipping
4 tablespoons skimmed milk
½ teaspoon salt
low fat cooking spray
¼ teaspoon ground cinnamon

 1 *ProPoints* value per serving
21 *ProPoints* values per recipe

C **47 calories** per serving

Takes **5 minutes** to prepare,
15 minutes to bake

V

✱ recommended

1 Preheat the oven to Gas Mark 3/160°C/fan oven 140°C.

2 Place all the ingredients, except the extra sugar, cooking spray and cinnamon, in a large bowl and combine well to form a smooth batter.

3 Spray a doughnut baking tray with the cooking spray. Half fill each doughnut mould with the batter mixture.

4 Bake for 10–15 minutes, until risen and firm to the touch. Be careful as the bottom of the doughnuts brown faster than the tops.

5 Meanwhile, on a small plate, mix together the dipping sugar and the cinnamon. Remove the cooked doughnuts from the tray one at a time and dip the bottom of each into the sugar and cinnamon mixture then leave to cool on a wire rack.

Coffee Cup Cakes

These little coffee flavoured cup cakes, served with an espresso syrup, are ideal as a dinner party dessert.

Makes 12

125 g (4½ oz) low fat spread
125 g (4½ oz) caster sugar
1 teaspoon vanilla extract
1 egg
150 g (5½ oz) self raising flour
2 teaspoons instant coffee granules dissolved in 2 tablespoons boiling water
2 tablespoons skimmed milk

For the coffee syrup
200 ml (7 fl oz) strong black coffee
100 g (3½ oz) caster sugar
1 tablespoon coffee liqueur (optional)

---

4 **ProPoints** values per serving
53 **ProPoints** values per recipe

205 **calories** per serving

Takes **5 minutes** to prepare, **20 minutes** to bake

V

* recommended

1 Preheat the oven to Gas Mark 4/180°C/fan oven 160°C. Place 12 cup cake cases in a muffin tray.

2 In a bowl, cream together the low fat spread and sugar until light and fluffy. Add the vanilla extract and egg and beat well.

3 Fold in the flour, coffee and milk. Place a tablespoon of the mixture into each cake case and bake for 15–20 minutes until a skewer inserted into the centre of one cake comes out clean and they are risen and golden.

4 For the coffee syrup, place the coffee, sugar and liqueur, if using, in a saucepan over a low heat and stir until the sugar has dissolved. Allow the syrup to boil for 5 minutes until it thickens.

5 To serve, remove the cakes from their cases, put on separate plates and pour the syrup over.

Tip These cup cakes will keep for a few days in an airtight container.

Cranberry and Almond Cookies

These little cookies are soft and chewy when still warm, then they crisp up as they cool. Store in an airtight container.

Makes 16

100 g (3½ oz) clear honey
50 g (1¾ oz) low fat spread
60 g (2 oz) dried cranberries
15 g (½ oz) flaked almonds
80 g (3 oz) porridge oats
80 g (3 oz) self raising flour
low fat cooking spray

---

2 *ProPoints* values per serving
37 *ProPoints* values per recipe

85 calories per serving

Takes **10 minutes** to prepare + cooling,
10 minutes to bake

V

✱ not recommended

1 Preheat the oven to Gas Mark 4/180°C/fan oven 160°C.

2 Put the honey and low fat spread in a small pan and heat gently until melted.

3 Mix the cranberries, almonds, porridge oats and flour together in a bowl, then pour in the honey mixture. Stir to bring together.

4 Spray a non stick baking tray with the cooking spray and spoon on the mixture in 16 mounds. Flatten slightly with the back of a spoon.

5 Bake for 10 minutes until set and golden brown, then cool on a wire rack.

Apple and Cinnamon Flapjacks

Apple and cinnamon is a classic combination, adding a delicious twist to these sweet flapjacks

Makes 12

100 g (3½ oz) low fat spread
75 g (2¾ oz) dark muscovado sugar
2 tablespoons golden syrup
175 g (6 oz) porridge oats
1 teaspoon ground cinnamon
75 g (2¾ oz) dried apple chunks, chopped into
  bite size pieces
25 g (1 oz) raisins or currants

---

4 ProPoints values per serving
49 ProPoints values per recipe

139 calories per serving

Takes **10 minutes** to prepare,
15 minutes to bake

V

✳ recommended

1 Preheat the oven to Gas Mark 5/190°C/fan oven 170°C. Line an 18 cm (7 inch) shallow, square tin with baking parchment.

2 Put the low fat spread, sugar and syrup in a large, heavy based pan and heat gently, stirring occasionally, until melted and well blended.

3 Mix in the oats, cinnamon, apple pieces and raisins or currants.

4 Spread the mixture into the prepared tin, level the top then bake for 15 minutes. Leave to cool in the tin before cutting into 12 squares. Once completely cold, remove from the tin and store in an airtight container for up to a week.

Orange Petticoat Tails

These little biscuits make a good accompaniment to a cup of tea. They will keep in an airtight container for up to a week.

Makes 12 wedges

200 g (7 oz) low fat spread
4 tablespoons artificial sweetener
40 g (1½ oz) caster sugar
50 g (1¾ oz) ground rice
grated zest of a large orange
200 g (7 oz) plain flour

4 _ProPoints_ values per serving
49 _ProPoints_ values per recipe

155 calories per serving

Takes **10 minutes** to prepare,
15 minutes to bake

V

✳ not recommended

1 Preheat the oven to Gas Mark 4/180°C/fan oven 160°C and line a baking tray with baking parchment.

2 Place the low fat spread, sweetener, sugar, ground rice and orange zest in a large bowl and mix with a fork until thoroughly combined.

3 Add the flour by sprinkling it over and incorporating it with your fingertips to form a dough.

4 Place the dough on the baking sheet and roll or pat out to a 5 mm (¼ inch) thick circle. Using a sharp knife, score lines out from a centre point (do not cut all the way through) like spokes on a wheel to make 12 small wedges. Bake for 15 minutes, until golden brown.

5 To serve, slice up the biscuit into the 12 wedges.

Tip It helps to keep the mixture cool or it may become too sticky. The mixture can be refrigerated for 10 minutes or so before rolling out if it is too difficult to handle.

Ground rice is available from the baking section of most supermarkets. It cooks quickly and adds texture to these biscuits.

Index